T0090589

Cambridge Elements ≡

Elements in Publishing and Book Culture
edited by
Samantha Rayner
University College London
Leah Tether
University of Bristol

THE EARLY DEVELOPMENT OF PROJECT GUTENBERG C.1970–2000

Simon Rowberry
University College London

CAMBRIDGE
UNIVERSITY PRESS

Shaftesbury Road, Cambridge CB2 8EA, United Kingdom

One Liberty Plaza, 20th Floor, New York, NY 10006, USA

477 Williamstown Road, Port Melbourne, VIC 3207, Australia

314–321, 3rd Floor, Plot 3, Splendor Forum, Jasola District Centre,
New Delhi – 110025, India

103 Penang Road, #05–06/07, Visioncrest Commercial, Singapore 238467

Cambridge University Press is part of Cambridge University Press & Assessment,
a department of the University of Cambridge.

We share the University's mission to contribute to society through the pursuit of
education, learning and research at the highest international levels of excellence.

www.cambridge.org
Information on this title: www.cambridge.org/9781108743181

DOI: 10.1017/9781108785778

First published 2023

A catalogue record for this publication is available from the British Library.

ISBN 978-1-108-74318-1 Paperback
ISSN 2514-8524 (online)
ISSN 2514-8516 (print)

The Early Development of Project Gutenberg c.1970–2000

Elements in Publishing and Book Culture

DOI: 10.1017/9781108785778

First published online: June 2023

Simon Rowberry

University College London

Author for correspondence: Simon Rowberry, s.rowberry@ucl.ac.uk

ABSTRACT: Project Gutenberg is lauded as one of the earliest digitisation initiatives, a mythology that Michael Hart, its founder perpetuated through to his death in 2011. In this Element, the author re-examines the extant historical evidence to challenge some of Hart's bolder claims and resituates the significance of Project Gutenberg in relation to broader trends in online document delivery and digitisation in the latter half of the twentieth century, especially in the World Wide Web's first decade (the 1990s). Through this re-appraisal, the author instead suggests that Hart's Project is significant as an example of what Millicent Weber has termed a "digital publishing collective" whereby a group of volunteers engage in producing content and that process is as meaningful as the final product.

KEYWORDS: digital publishing, digitisation, e-books, Project Gutenberg, history of computing

ISBNs: 9781108743181 (PB), 9781108785778 (OC)

ISSNs: 2514-8524 (online), 2514-8516 (print)

Contents

1 Introduction

The September 2011 *New York Times* obituary for Michael Stern Hart claimed that he had 'laid the foundations for Project Gutenberg, the oldest and largest digital library'.[1] The obituary recites what I term the 'Standard Narrative', set up by Hart's 1992 document, 'The History and Philosophy of Project Gutenberg':[2] On 4 July 1971, Hart was inspired to digitise a copy of the US *Declaration of Independence* that he had received while grocery shopping. He achieved this through his student access to the University of Illinois at Urbana-Champaign's (UIUC) Xerox Sigma V, an early computer launched in 1967. He valued his use of the time-sharing network at $100 million (he never provided calculations), which he wanted to use in the most effective way for society's benefit.[3] From this moment on, Hart vocally advocated for reading on-screen until his death.

According to Hart, users would access the texts through ARPANET, a military computer network seen as a precursor to the Internet, through UIUC's local connection. As the Internet matured, Hart moved his operations to the most promising platform on the Internet as users moved between rival protocols in the early 1990s. Finally, the mainstream acceptance of the Web gave the Project a permanent home that, along with an increase in the number of volunteers, ensured the Project's longer-term sustainability.

Even in an era dominated by commercial mass digitisation projects and e-book stores including Google Books and the Kindle, Project Gutenberg offers an impressive 65,000 e-books as of April 2021, showing a steady interest from both volunteers and consumers. Between 1971 and 2021, several milestones in digital publishing encouraged reading on-screen including the World Wide Web in 1989, and the launch of the Kindle in 2007. Nonetheless Hart maintained his original vision, advocating for freely available, simple plain text publications and reusability over profit or readability as a document. Through this approach, he imparted an idealised digitisation imagination while simultaneously reenforcing the pitfalls of

---

[1] Grimes, 'Michael Hart'. [2] Hart, 'The History and Philosophy'.
[3] Hart, 'The History and Philosophy'.

mass digitisation projects such as Google Books with regard to curatorial biases.

Hart's 'standard narrative' has become central to our understanding of the historical development of e-books but has rarely been critically interrogated. This approach leads to blind spots, especially in terms of representation. This Element seeks to address these blind spots through refocusing the narrative around Project Gutenberg. While Hart is a central figure in the history of Project Gutenberg, this Element is not his biography. Instead, I focus on systems and collaborations that led to the success of the Project that often extended beyond Hart's control. The history of Project Gutenberg instead reflects the contours of the broader social and technical histories of the development of the Internet, from a small, elite group of academics through to crowdsourcing in the early twenty-first century. This is not a story of exceptionalism but rather one of many emerging data points about the uptake of the personal computer in the twentieth century that focuses on textual production and consumption.

Figure 1 shows the rapid growth of Project Gutenberg between the late 1990s and 2003 as well as the slow, steady decline in publications since the late 2000s.[4] The two highest peaks represent a surge in interest in e-books during the early 2000s and then the later response to the emergence of a stable e-book ecosystem with the launch of the Kindle in 2007. The decline in publications since 2010 is complex and cannot be reduced to the common suggestion of a supposed recent decline in interest around e-books. There is a hard limit to the labour and materials available for Project Gutenberg's operations, as I discuss in Chapters 4 and 5, which created this bottleneck.

The Project focused on publishing titles in the public domain, free from the restrictions of the copyright system, although there were some early exceptions. Hart drew from both public domain titles published before the 1920s and therefore no longer protected by copyright, as well as more contemporary titles without copyright including government publications (CIA World Factbooks, the US Census, the North American Free Trade

---

[4] The large rise in publications in 2020 and 2021 may reflect more users volunteering during the COVID-19 pandemic, a response to new titles entering the public domain, or both.

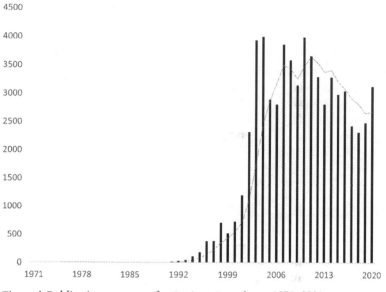

Figure 1 Publications per year for Project Gutenberg. 1971–2021

Agreement), resources for early Web users, the human genome, and long strings of significant irrational numbers. It is challenging to identify public domain material that is accessible outside of academic and research library special collections. The public domain is a flexible concept. After a lengthy 'freezing' of new titles entering the public domain, new works were included from 2018. The dip in the 2010s represents a bottleneck in available material followed by the expansion of the public domain. Despite the slight decline from the peak, the graph overall shows a level of stability within the Project due to its professionalisation in the 1990s.

    Project Gutenberg's expansion after 2000 is beyond the scope of this Element. This is not a problem, however, as its exponential growth between 2000 and 2003 was the result of Hart's groundwork over the previous decade. My end date of 2000 also separates the early experimental years of digital publishing from its increased commercialisation over the following decade. The volume of new publications post-2000 also requires a shift from the manual data collection underpinning this project to automated computational analysis given the Project's exponential growth. Once a larger audience started to become interested in e-books, more historically significant data was generated and recorded. Conversely, the early years of digital publishing are less well known as the numbers reporting on the ground were much smaller.

Through focusing on Project Gutenberg's formative development, I have two main aims: (1) offer a revisionist narrative around the early development of e-book culture through the lens of Project Gutenberg; and (2) to demonstrate the importance of a stronger historiographical approach to digital publishing. Through this analysis, I decouple myth from fact to demonstrate that the historiography of early e-books is a worthwhile avenue of exploration for two main reasons: First, as with many aspects of the history of technology, the field is dominated by heroic narratives of great men from Anglophone countries rather than recognising the more diverse origin stories of these technologies. Second, a greater understanding of the longer, deeper history of digital publishing helps recontextualise the contemporary moment: What does it mean if the early milestones of e-book history are much earlier than typically expected? Why have these narratives been portrayed in the current way? In this Element, I aim to spark broader conversations around the intersection of digitisation and e-book historiography with this case study. This Element examines Project Gutenberg's importance for forming the popular imagination of community book digitisation and how its ad hoc governance had consequences for the types of materials broadly available before the wider uptake of mass digitisation. To this end, I build upon Bonnie Mak and Stephen Gregg's in-depth investigations of Early English Books Online and Eighteenth Century Collections Online respectively.[5] As these previous case studies show, balancing both the technical and social challenges ensures a deeper understanding of digital publishing's history rather than viewing either in isolation.

---

[5] Mak, 'Archaeology of a Digitization'; Gregg, *Old Books*.

Beyond critical digitisation studies, this Element also draws upon emerging discussions around labour and collaboration in digital publishing. Millicent Weber offers the useful concept of the 'digital publishing collective' in her discussion of LibriVox, a website that produces public domain audiobooks, often from the Project Gutenberg editions. She argues that:

> describing these spaces as collectives refers to the independent and idealistic ways they are organised, deriving from their volunteer-driven ethos, the concept of the 'digital publishing collective' is designed to maintain a sense of critical caution in relation to such idealism.[6]

We can identify some of these traits in Project Gutenberg but we must proceed with caution with a platform built on a heroic founder mythology rather than emphasising a more decentralised approach to leadership and direction. In reality, the Project required this collaborative network but it was not outwardly presented in this light before 2000. Nonetheless, Project Gutenberg demonstrates the inherent contradictions between the outward facing lone genius model when coupled with a more collaborative digital publishing collective approach behind the scenes.

A final strand of disciplinary influence comes from the intersection between media studies, the history of computing, and platform studies. I engage with the recent turn towards revisionist histories within proto-Internet studies as outlined in Joy Lisi Rankin's *A People's History of Computing in the United States* and Kevin Driscoll's *The Modem World*, which have challenged the long-held orthodoxies about how non-academic users engaged with each other in national and transnational networks prior to the mainstream acceptance of the Web.[7] This Element complements this research by exploring how this underacknowledged historical era, especially outside of elite accounts, has led to the development of folklore that requires further contextualisation.

---

[6] Weber, '"Reading" the Public Domain': 216.

[7] Lisi Rankin, *A People's History of Computing*; Driscoll, *Modem World*.

1.1 A Note on Methods

E-book historiography before the Kindle is difficult to research, as primary sources are often dispersed and hidden within larger archives. Nonetheless, closer scrutiny of extant contemporaneous sources challenges Hart's Standard Narrative. As a born-digital project, primary sources for Project Gutenberg are dispersed across institutional archives and the Web, many of which are only partially reconstructed as what Niels Brügger calls 'reborn-digital material [. . .] that has to a large extent been changed in the process of collecting and preserving'.[8] For example, since a webpage may rely on a database and assemble media files from several different servers, the archived version cannot be an accurate representation of the original. The challenge is compounded by the scarcity of relevant born-digital data available prior to 1990. As a result, my data provides an incomplete picture of Project Gutenberg's early years but nonetheless, this partial data reveals enough to challenge the Standard Narrative. As born-digital preservation becomes the norm rather than the exception within archives, the accession of more personal records may illuminate further details on Project Gutenberg's formative years through evidence that is not currently publicly available.[9] Through this extended case study, I aim to provide some broader suggestions for developing a historiographical approach to e-books through navigating extant born-digital records that may be enhanced through future archival accessions.

My primary sources included archived mailing lists (Book People, Humanist), Usenet groups (bit.listserv.gutnberg, www-talk), reborn-digital archives (Internet Archive, the Michael S. Hart Archives), e-book aggregators (various Project Gutenberg websites, Textfiles, the Internet Archive, Oxford Text Archives), and physical archives at Stanford University Library. The born-digital archives present unique challenges that shape the historical record. For example, the Book People mailing list ran on an instance of Brent Chapman's Majordomo, a suite of tools for

---

[8] Brügger, 'Digital Humanities in the 21st Century'.

[9] There is a growing body of scholarship on the impact of born-digital material's arrival in archives including Kirschenbaum, 'The Txtual Condition'; Brügger, 'Web Historiography and Internet Studies'; Langdon, 'Describing the Digital'; Özdemir, 'The Inevitability of Digital Transfer'.

managing email mailing lists automatically, which redacts email addresses in its archives, rendering some identities difficult to recover. Michael Hart's born-digital papers include his email correspondence between 1993 and 1995, but there is little evidence of networks towards the latter half of the decade. This cache of several thousand emails was a boon for reconstructing historical events but many emails were corrupt or conjoined into lengthy threads that shift between topics. Likewise, Project Gutenberg titles feature incomplete bibliographic histories, and the main site and its mirrors will only show the last version of a text. Unfortunately, given the lack of version control and reuploads, most metadata around publication dates and versions are unreliable and therefore there may be discrepancies in my account. Where possible, I have used the versions in Project Gutenberg's 'Old' folder which are closer to the original although there is some evidence these documents have also been altered through the publication dates.

1.2 Book Overview

My argument in this Element splits into two main topics, which form the structure of the chapters. Chapters 2 and 3, 'Mythological Origins' and 'Ideology', tackle Hart and Project Gutenberg's pre-existing hagiography as outlined in Hart's 'History and Philosophy'. This essential first step outlines why viewing Hart as a lone genius only offers a limited perspective on the Project's development while acknowledging that the founder remains a central figure in its historical development. 'Mythological Origins' contrasts Hart's claims about his work between 1971 and 1989 with the substantial evidence of other groups working on more sophisticated projects both prior to and during this time. The third chapter, 'Ideology', turns to what convinced Hart to launch Project Gutenberg and how he used it as a vehicle for his own views on the future of digital media. I also highlight how cultivating a lone genius mythology might have backfired on the Project when Hart began to fight with academics on mailing lists.

Chapters 4–7 shift focus to the collaborative aspects of the Project through a dual analytical frame of platform studies and digital publishing collectives, which emphasise the technological and social over individual's achievements. I use these two theoretical positions to nuance our understandings of platforms as either corporatised social media networks or technological infrastructure for further innovation. Instead, I question if Project Gutenberg's looser structure should be considered a mixture between a platform and a digital collective that I term an 'anti-platform' in the final chapter. The fourth chapter, 'Technological Platforms', focuses on the importance of the Web and related technologies to the Project's rapid growth in the 1990s. Chapter 5, 'Platform Governance', explores platforms from a sociological perspective, suggesting that the increased professionalisation in running the Project, along with acclimatation to multiple changes to copyright law that accounted for the rise of the Web, shaped the course of PG over the 1990s. 'Digital Publishing Collective', the sixth chapter, zooms in from the platform to consider the impact of contributors and volunteers in shaping the content available on the Project. Through Hart's laisse-faire attitude towards digitisation, significant oversights continued to be a problem in the curation of material.

The final chapter, 'Anti-Platform: Project Gutenberg's Lasting Influence', reassesses my previous framing of Project Gutenberg as a platform through considering the memetic qualities of the Project since the early 2000s. If it is more of a collective and volunteer base than a platform or infrastructure, content can easily be reused in various contexts. Rather than consolidating influence as a central repository for public domain digitisations, the Project has instead dissipated, becoming the base for many other initiatives, in the face of well-resourced mass digitisation projects such as the Internet Archive and Google Books. In the current context, Project Gutenberg's mythology has become all-consuming in its narrative. Nonetheless, through this re-examination, I aim to demonstrate the importance of the Project lies in its development of a community rather than simply relying on metrics of content acquisition and publication.

2 Mythological Origins

2.1 Introduction

Michael Hart's 'History and Philosophy' provided the foundations for the Project Gutenberg mythology that he was keen to cultivate. He was not the first to digitise books for consumption on-screen, but the name Project Gutenberg is synonymous with community book digitisation, while similar contemporary initiatives such as the Oxford Text Archive are less well known.[10] Why has Project Gutenberg remained so prominent in the public and academic imagination in the era of Google Books, HathiTrust and the Kindle? Its position can partially be attributed to its acceptance in what Thomas Streeter calls the 'standard folklore' of the Internet, the established series of stories that are commonly recited about how the Internet came into existence.[11] The folklore is comprehensive, so I instead focus here on just a singular narrative around Hart's position.

In this chapter, I challenge the Standard Narrative of Project Gutenberg's rise through analysing earlier digitisation projects dating back to the 1950s, and the relative stagnation of Hart's Project until 1989. Hart undoubtedly found success by the mid-1990s, noting that 'sales of a Gutenberg CD-ROM [. . .] hit 100,000 copies' in 1997, but this was far from guaranteed at the beginning of the 1990s.[12] Hart was just one of many individuals working on digitisation before the mainstream acceptance of the Web in the late 1990s, and he was undertaking this work without the backing of an elite academic institution.

Through my analysis in this chapter and the following chapter, I draw upon Robert Merton's framework of 'singletons', or lone inventors, and 'multiples', discoveries that occur simultaneously which can lead to contested claims of innovation within the history of science.[13] Classic examples

---

[10] For further scholarship on digital community digitisation, see Terras, 'Digital Curiosities'; Oomen and Aroyo, 'Crowdsourcing in the Cultural Heritage Domain'; Ridge, *Crowdsourcing Our Cultural Heritage*.

[11] Streeter, *Net Effect*, 22.   [12] Hamilton, 'Hart of the Gutenberg Galaxy'.

[13] Merton, 'Singletons and Multiples'.

of 'multiples' include Isaac Newton and Gottfried Wilhelm Leibniz's contested simultaneous invention of infinitesimal calculus, as well as Alfred Russel Wallace and Charles Darwin's theories of evolution. Dean Simonton advances, but does not commit to, the '*zeitgeist* theory of creativity', a 'social deterministic view' whereby the right conditions for an invention increase the potential for simultaneous discovery while not discounting the nature of genius required to make that step.[14] Within intellectual property debates, this is the equivalent that an invention protected by a patent is considered 'non-obvious'.[15]

The 'singletons' view can promote what Ralph Epstein calls the 'heroic' model of history and I call the 'lone genius' myth.[16] In the case of the history of computing, the lone genius myth can be pervasive because of the lack of contradictory evidence due to archival collection processes, as is the case with Project Gutenberg. As with his contemporaries in the history of computing including Steve Jobs and Bill Gates, Hart leveraged the mythology of the lone genius. Joy Lisi Rankin argues that this 'mythology does us a disservice. It creates a digital America dependent on the work of a handful of male tech geniuses. It deletes the work of the many individuals who had been computing, and it effaces their diversity'.[17] My archival research is limited by the extant available material that centres Hart as the founder but, nonetheless, email and other documented interactions begin to decentre his position in favour of a more collaborative effort.

Mailing lists are one such source that offers a broader perspective. One of Hart's favourite mailing lists was Humanist, founded in 1987 to discuss what was then known as humanities computing. The Humanist archives feature evidence of an alternative to the standard narrative from Hart, who used the mailing list to publicly launch the rejuvenated Project in August 1989 with a message calling for participants:

---

[14] Simonton, 'Multiple Discovery and Invention', 1603.

[15] USPTO, '2141 Examination Guidelines'.

[16] Epstein, 'Industrial Invention', 237.

[17] Lisi Rankin, *People's History of Computing*, 3.

ANNOUNCEMENT OF NEW DISCUSSION GROUP
SUBJECT: ELECTRONIC TEXTS, THEIR CREATION
AND DISTRIBUTION

> With the generous assistance of the University of Illinois,
> I am proud to announce the public opening of Project
> Gutenberg. The purpose of Project Gutenberg is to promote
> the distribution and creation of electronic texts.[18]

This was one of the first times that Project Gutenberg was articulated in
such a clear way in public. Indeed, there is very little extant evidence of
a 'Project Gutenberg' prior to 1989. An earlier post in June 1989 revealed an
entirely different business model:

> Current projects include putting the Great Books into
> machine readable form, plus an unabridged dictionary.
> Plans are to charge a truly minimal fee such as $1 for
> materials up to 150Kb, for larger files add $1 per 100Kb.
> Fifteen years have gone into this project, which I will view
> as personally completed when we have released 10,000 $1
> volumes of the highest quality[19]

There is no evidence that Hart ever implemented this payment scheme,
which would have been a hallmark of early Bulletin Board Systems (BBSs)
that required a user to manually dial in to the server. The shift to FTP
servers and Usenet, documented further in Chapter 4, ensured that this plan
was never implemented.

Given the immaturity of Internet infrastructure and Hart's lack of
institutional resources before his relaunch in 1989, it was difficult for the
Project to have a significant online presence. Between 1971 and 1989, Hart

---

[18] Michael S. Hart to Humanist Discussion Group, '3.421: Form for Discussion of
Electronic Texts', 31 August 1989.

[19] Hart quoted in Willard McCarty to Humanist Discussion Group, '3.171:
Biographical Supplement 19', 25 June 1989.

published nine texts, largely pivotal documents authored by the US founding fathers, consisting of 16,000 words (or c.900 words per year), short of
the length of most conventional novels. By contrast, the Project Gutenberg
King James Bible clocked in at 800,000 words. The documents digitised
prior to the *King James Bible* could have been achieved by a reasonably fast
typist over a couple of days, while the Bible represented a step change in
Hart's ambitions. Justin Peters suggests that before 1989, 'to the extent
[Project Gutenberg] existed at all, [it] was a hobby, intermittently pursued,
fated for obscurity'.[20] The Michael S. Hart papers feature major gaps
between him graduating from University and ramping up Project
Gutenberg activities in the mid-to-late 1980s. In this formative time, the
Project was not a priority and some attempts to produce longer outputs led
to discarded failures such as an early effort to digitise the complete works of
Shakespeare during the 1980s or the complete works of James Joyce in 1993
that were both denied by their problematic copyright statuses.[21] This early
endeavour emphasised the dual nature of labour for the Project: first, the
visible work of digitising books, but second, the equally important but
invisible labour of ensuring the material is suitable for publication.

2.2 Was Michael Hart the First to Digitise a Text?

Hart's early solo work on Project Gutenberg on a nascent Internet is
impressive, but he was part of a larger movement to digitise texts in the
early decades of the digital computer. His claims about PG's early influence
across digitisation communities therefore need further contextualisation.
Hart acknowledged that there were earlier examples of digitisation for local
computational analysis, but he claimed that Project Gutenberg was instead
the first effort focused on *distribution* for reading. He boasted that after
extensive research, he had never encountered a publicly available e-book
released before July 1971.[22] Despite these claims, Hart admitted that only

---

[20] Peters, *The Idealist*, 105.

[21] Murphy, *Shakespeare in Print*, 333; Poynder and Hart, 'Preserving the Public
      Domain', 10; Jason Eisner to Michael S. Hart, 'Complete Works of Joyce:
      Further Info', 22 April 1993.

[22] Hart, 'Who.Invented.Ebooks.Txt'.

six network users accessed the *Declaration of Independence* in the Project's early years, but he 'was convinced that he had hit on something big, even if, or perhaps *because*, no one else shared his optimism'.[23] To the contrary, academics and cultural heritage institutions had already developed infrastructure. Furthermore, the range of related projects focusing on text and computing detailed below demonstrate that Hart was working within the 'zeitgeist' model of creativity, where it was self-evident that computers could be used to transmit text. In the rest of this chapter, I outline four different initiatives that were working on similar projects by the 1970s.

2.2.1 Early Information Retrieval Systems

As early as the 1960s, several companies and start-ups were already exploring the possibilities of transmitting text over both local and national networks, especially within the context of professional and reference publishing. Charles P. Bourne and Trudi Bellardo Hahn's *A History of Online Information Services, 1963-1976* offers a comprehensive overview of this work, but I want to highlight three pre-1971 examples from their work that shows the breadth of experimentation from that period. First, NASA started looking for an external developer for 'a prototype online system to employ the full NASA document collection (about 200,000), in a realistic library environment for direct use by scientists and engineers' as early as 1965.[24] Likewise, the US Patent Office started working on digitisation and network transmission of patent documents in 1967 with a working prototype by December 1971.[25] Finally, work on LEXIS, the legal text database, started in 1966 for the Ohio Bar group with a functional product in circulation by 1970.[26] These three examples, and the many other similar projects undertaken in the same period, were aimed at a different market: professional use where quick retrieval and skimming were important. Long-form reading on-screen was a greater challenge that required specialised equipment and infrastructure to be successful.

---

[23] Hart never specified when these users accessed the text. Peters, *The Idealist*, 97.

[24] Bourne and Hahn, *A History of Online Information Services*, 156.

[25] Bourne and Hahn, 107. [26] Bourne and Hahn, 236–50.

Many of these early projects' histories are less well known than Project Gutenberg even if their current forms, such as Lexis Nexis, are more popular. Nonetheless, an early focus on infrastructure rather than content acquisition ensured the long-term sustainability of these initiatives. Conversely, Project Gutenberg largely depended on digitising content and hoping others would develop the infrastructure until the mid-1990s. Without investing in the infrastructure it is impossible to reach a certain scale or usefulness, and the Project was largely hampered by waiting for others, such as Tim Berners-Lee or other early contributors to the Web, to construct the infrastructure necessary to share large volumes of text online. Therefore, the efforts by others were more instrumental in the long-term success of reading on-screen.

2.2.2 Early Digital Humanities Projects

Beyond early commercial systems, other academic initiatives focused on text digitisation within the nascent digital humanities community. Histories of digital humanities often start with Roberto Busa's digitisation of the works of Thomas Aquinas, coordinated by female punch card operatives, as an origin story, dating back to the 1940s.[27] While this may be one of the earliest extant examples, it was far from the only digitisation project active before 1971. In fact, when PG restarted in 1989, it was one of over 250 projects identified by the *Georgetown Catalog of Projects in Electronic Text*.[28] Some of these projects were active around or before the start of Project Gutenberg.

As with many aspects of the early history of computing, there is only limited evidence remaining for these pre-PG projects but early digitisers were keen to share their progress in academic journals and other fora. Most prominently, the early digital humanities journal, *Computers and the Humanities*, started in 1967 as a forum for early work in the field, compiled a list of 'Literary Works in Machine-Readable Form'. These articles featured lists of work-in-progress and completed digitisations that might

---

[27] Terras and Nyhan, 'Father Busa's Female Punch Card Operatives'.

[28] Michael Neuman to Humanist Discussion Group, '3.1095: Georgetown Catalog of Projects in Electronic Text', 22 February 1990.

be of interest to others along with contact details for copies, which would primarily be distributed via the postal service using tape reels. This list offers a useful insight into the sorts of activities happening prior to PG's launch. I cannot claim that this data source is authoritative, but given the deeply uneven distribution of computers internationally in the 1960s, this sample unfortunately may be representative of global digitisation activity.

The list of publishers reveals a consolidation of interests at a handful of institutions rather than the full diversity of projects. For example in the 1967 'Literary Works in Machine-Readable Form', Bertrand Augst from the University of California-Berkeley covers thirty of the ninety texts ranging from contemporary plays by Eugene Ionesco and Samuel Beckett through to the sermons of St. Bernard and Charles Baudelaire's *Les Fleurs du mal*.[29] Other major research universities, often pioneers within the fields of digital humanities and information science, including Cambridge, Michigan, Brown, Virginia, Texas-Austin, and Toronto, are also present on the list. Early digitisation projects were the domain of these large research-intensive universities. Richer institutions dominate the lists, even in cases where initial appearances suggest otherwise. For example, Sister Dolores Marie Burton from the women-only Emmanuel College in Boston conducted an early digitisation of William Shakespeare, but she completed this work while a PhD student at Harvard.[30]

From this early cross-section of institutional digitisation labour, there is already a clear divide between the research-intensive universities who were able to commit to this work and those working outside or at the fringes of the academy who were not represented through *CHum*'s listings. Project Gutenberg offered a productive channel for those working outside of institutions, although as Kevin Driscoll notes, ARPANET remained an elite network while non-academic users would often use Bulletin Board Systems (BBSes) and other dial-up arrangements rather than the emerging Internet until the late 1990s.[31] There is limited evidence that Project Gutenberg was available on these other networks, but this could largely be the result of the lack of archival evidence rather than historical facts.

---

[29] Carlson, 'Literary Works in Machine-Readable Form'.
[30] Murphy, *Shakespeare in Print*, 325. [31] Driscoll, *Modem World*, 9.

It was only with a shift in thinking in the mid-1980s that any of these institutions, including PG started to consider a broader audience for consuming this text.

2.2.3 The Oxford Text Archive

The early humanities computing community grew rapidly during the 1970s and 1980s leading to a plethora of digitised texts during the early years of Project Gutenberg. The first International Conference on Computing in the Humanities, the precursor to the Association for Digital Humanities, occurred in 1971 and the community grew rapidly.[32] The Oxford Text Archive (OTA), originally called the Oxford Archive of English Literature, is the most visible remnant of this era and collected academic digitisations between its launch in 1976 and Project Gutenberg's re-emergence in 1989. The anonymously authored 1592 play *Arden of Feversham*, digitised by the University of Oxford in 1971, and William Shakespeare's *King Henry VI Pt 2* were the first two documents uploaded to the archive, indicating the sort of material the OTA curated in its formational years. A 1979 announcement of the Archive in *CHum* stated its objective as 'to establish and maintain an archive of machine-readable texts of English Literature'.[33] In a retrospective on the OTA's role within humanities computing, Susan Hockey noted it was intended to maintain digitised texts that might otherwise be abandoned by their creators.[34]

The Oxford Text Archive's institutional legitimacy was solidified by its appointment 'as one of five Service Providers for the UK-based, national Arts and Humanities Data Service' in 1996.[35] As a result, the OTA enjoyed a level of support that encouraged academics to deposit their ad hoc digitised texts. The OTA's Legacy Collection reveals the extent of early activity with 760 texts uploaded between 1976 and 1986. Many of these texts are encoded using arcane, proprietary formats such as OCP, files developed for analysis through the Oxford Concordance

---

[32] Eichmann-Kalwara et al., 'Association for Computers'.

[33] 'Directory of Scholars Active', 363.

[34] Hockey, 'The History of Humanities Computing', 8.

[35] Morrison, 'Delivering Electronic Texts over the Web'.

Program, which makes them difficult to read but nonetheless, that is over seventy-five times more texts than were available via Project Gutenberg during the same period.

Despite leveraging Oxford University's reputation, the OTA initially faced issues around professionalisation. In 1999, Alan Morrison admitted that depositing to OTA occurred in a largely ad hoc manner.[36] Without official policies, the OTA faced many of the same problems Project Gutenberg encountered in its early years. As Michael Neuman recalls, early entries into the OTA often ignored the realities of copyright, instead relying on fair use provision to ensure that scholars could access texts for research purposes.[37] This relaxed attitude was compatible with Hart's early approach to Project Gutenberg prior to 1989. Once networks started to formalise and grow due to the widespread adoption of protocols including FTP, Gopher, and the World Wide Web, there was less margin for error. If these texts were publicly accessible without using arcane protocols, copyright infringing material was more likely to be discovered. This marked a shift from samizdat distribution to more formalised mechanisms. It is noteworthy that institutional digitisation projects did not necessarily have better legal know-how than amateur projects such as Project Gutenberg, and both professionalised rapidly due to the increased audience I will discuss further in the next chapter.

2.2.4 PLATO

Beyond digitisation projects, we can also consider the range of networks available to Hart. The University of Illinois was a pioneer in early network computing through the development of PLATO (Programmed Logic for Automatic Teaching Operations), run by the University's Coordinated Science Laboratory starting in 1960. Joy Lisi Rankin suggests that PLATO offers a healthy corrective to the dominant narrative of Silicon Valley's role in the rise of computing, encouraging what she terms computing 'citizenship' over consumption. In Lisi Rankin's formulation, citizenship

---

[36] Morrison, 'Delivering Electronic Texts over the Web'.
[37] Neuman, 'The Very Pulse of the Machine', 368.

was a central pillar to the early acts of computing as users often played multiple roles in production, governance, and consumption on networks.[38]

In the 1965 final summary report to the US military, a major funder of the project, Bitzer et al. described their system with reference to 'electronic books', and an early preview of the system appeared in the Office of Naval Research's *Digital Computer Newsletter* in 1961.[39] While this alluded more to a notebook used in combination with an 'electronic blackboard' for a learning device, it represents one of the earliest known uses of the phrase. While none of Hart's extant contemporaneous accounts of Project Gutenberg's development features PLATO, Hart later suggested that by the 1980s, he was an active participant.[40] The Illinois context is vital for understanding the lack of Hart's institutionalisation: he worked on the fringes of developments at UIUC rather than with the initiatives that could have helped PG to scale earlier. This context also informs the sort of volunteer Hart was able to recruit into the Project outside of the core humanities computing community.

2.3 Hart's Shifting Narrative

Hart's bold claims to be the first to digitise a text to distribute it over a computer network were challenged on mailing lists. For example, in a July 2006 skirmish on the *Book People* mailing list, Hart defended the veracity of his connections to ARPANET. José Menéndez, a prominent digitiser for iBiblio, questioned Hart's narrative that he launched Project Gutenberg via ARPANET on 4 July 1971.[41] Menéndez built his argument on evidence that contradicted Hart's claims. A canonical map of all ARPANET nodes in August 1971 only shows a Digital Equipment Corporation (DEC) PDP-11 and Burroughs B6500 at Illinois.[42] This was corroborated with other evidence from early Network Work Group Requests for Comments (RFCs). It was clear, however, that a Xerox Sigma V was *not*

---

[38] Lisi Rankin, *A People's History of Computing*.

[39] Bitzer, Lyman, and Easley Jr., 'The Uses of Plato'; Goldstein, 'PLATO II'.

[40] Hart, 'Mt.Specifics.Txt'.

[41] José Menéndez to Book People mailing list, 'ARPANET Records', 29 June 2006.

[42] Heart et al., 'A History of the ARPANET', III–146.

connected to ARPANET in July 1971. Hart eventually conceded, 'I WAS told that 'WE' at the Xerox Sigma V had access to some new network via which we could and did send and receive messages and files from places I had to presume were the same sites as 'Internet' sites we heard about.'[43] It is therefore likely that Hart was sharing on one of a number of 'time-sharing' networks, where several users could simultaneously access a single central server through terminals, available at UIUC that used the PDP-11 or B6500, if not ARPANET itself. While the contemporary Internet primarily coalesced out of ARPANET, as the so-called network of networks, it is not so important which network Hart was sharing on as long as it was external. Indeed, as Ben Peters and Joy Lisi Rankin have shown, ARPANET was not the only pre-Internet network available by the 1970s either in the United States or globally.[44] For Hart, it was instead important that this was a proof-of-concept for how texts could be transmitted over a network.

Menéndez's second critical approach focused on anniversaries.[45] He uncovered several of Hart's earlier emails that claimed he digitised the Declaration of Independence in March 1971 such as a mailing to Humanist titled 'Riding the Growth Curve' in which he states 'our 21st anniversary on March 21, 1992', corroborated by the header of *Alice's Adventures in Wonderland*, which states 'this edition is being officially released on March 8, 1994 in celebration of the 23rd Anniversary of Project Gutenberg'.[46] The matter is further complicated by the currently available metadata for the first version of the 'Declaration of Independence' on Project Gutenberg, which states a publication date of 1 December 1971.[47]

---

[43] Michael S. Hart to Book People mailing list, 'Re: ARPANET Records (Fwd)', 12 July 2006.

[44] Lisi Rankin, *A People's History of Computing*; Peters, 'A Network Is Not a Network'.

[45] José Menéndez to Book People mailing list, 'Re: EXTRA! Project Gutenberg Weekly Newsletter', 5 July 2006.

[46] Michael S. Hart to Humanist Discussion Group, '5.0336 Project Gutenberg Update (1/90)', 22 September 1991; Carroll, 'Alice's Adventures in Wonderland'.

[47] Jefferson, 'The Declaration of Independence'.

Regardless of the date, others were already working on online texts prior to 1971. Hart's revisionist account prioritised mythology over accuracy. As Hart chose hagiography, he shifted the publication dates to suit his own narrative. Since any original evidence has been lost, the myths have become accepted as fact.

The choice of date was more symbolic than historically accurate, as it reenforced Hart's continual commitment to the Project through yearly milestones. The release dates for the first nine publications offer an alternative explanation for the December 1971 framing. The bibliographic metadata suggests that Hart published one document per year in December other than John F Kennedy's inaugural address which was released in November 1973. Each of these publications has the release date of the beginning of the month, a pattern that would continue with later publications that were months ahead of schedule, indicating Hart's aesthetic preference for dating publications. Releasing one short text per year reveals Hart's lack of resources to grow the Project.

Hart followed this pattern of one release per year until 1979, when he took a hiatus for a decade before the release of the *King James Bible* in 1989. The earliest extant correspondence relating to the Project available in Hart's papers dates back to 1985, so there is a missing half decade in the history of Project Gutenberg. It is unsurprising that the Project remained dormant for this period as it marks the transitionary moment between terminal computing, and the rise of the personal computer that facilitated the development of a much wider audience for Hart's work. The PC was far more compatible with the ideals of reading on screen in a leisurely environment, and with the introduction of portable computers by the 1980s, there were further possibilities for keen digitisers to explore.

2.4 Conclusion

There is a clear gap between how Hart framed Project Gutenberg in his 1992 'History and Philosophy' standard narrative and the extant contemporary evidence. Prior to 1989, the Project was dormant, and Hart required additional help to achieve his vision. Rather than focus on Hart's hagiographic claims, we can instead contextualise his achievements in relation to contemporaneous developments. Since Hart admit the Project did not 'publicly' launch until 1989, its longer history is contingent on relatively sparse evidence that he was an early pioneer, as opposed to the substantial evidence of others' work in the field since the 1960s. Hart and Project Gutenberg were lauded instead because of their longevity as much of this earlier work did not maintain the transition to the Web era unless it received major corporate funding. When considering this hagiography, it is worth explaining why it was so important for Hart to claim these milestones rather than offer a more nuanced history of the Project.

3 Ideology

Hart's decision to build Project Gutenberg was not altruistic. Instead, he was driven by deeply held ideological convictions around free access to plain text files initially for computational analysis, and later for consumption by the public. Once these efforts started to gain traction he pivoted towards recognition for his individual achievements. This shift reflects other cases of the 'Lone Genius' myth. Unfortunately, this set up tensions within digital humanities circles, especially those working on text encoding such as the Oxford Text Archive (OTA) and Text Encoding Initiative (TEI) communities, when Hart decided to prioritise plain text over other emerging file formats. As a result, Hart's status of the lone genius threatened the reputation of his Project which would only be remedied through embracing the collaborative approach that emerged over the 1990s. Before considering how Hart's strong ideology could have challenged the Project's success, it is worth pausing to consider Hart's position.

3.1 Leveraging Johannes Gutenberg's Reputation

Given the emphasis on mythology, what exactly was Hart hoping to get out of his efforts? In a document celebrating the 'first million e-books' (defined by the potential number of downloads rather than unique titles), Hart proclaimed: 'The goal of Project Gutenberg was "Neo-Mass Production", in an effort to create a "Neo-Industrial Revolution" that will bring as much more to the average person as did Gutenberg's printing press and the following 'Scientific and Industrial Revolutions' it caused.'[48] Project Gutenberg was far from a neutral repository in Hart's view as it was an important vehicle for his ideology. His writings beyond Project Gutenberg demonstrate that he subscribed to an optimistic form of technological determinism, or the belief that technology such as the printing press or the Internet fundamentally change society rather than acting as a tool for broader socially driven change. In the case of PG, distributing the books online would be sufficient for the public good.

---

[48]   Hart, 'First.Million.Ebooks.Txt'.

In many respects, Michael Hart replicated the success of his Project's namesake, Johannes Gutenberg, through claiming to be the first despite contradictory evidence. While Johannes Gutenberg is often credited as inventing movable type printing, the technology was instead already four centuries old in China.[49] Neither profited from their ideas in their lifetimes. Gutenberg divested the commercial aspects of his printing press to Johann Fust; Hart never commercialised Project Gutenberg and was largely overtaken by other large-scale digitisation projects such as the Internet Archive and Google Books.[50] Adrian Johns takes the Gutenberg narrative even further, suggesting that the 'orthodoxy' is based on scant corroborating documents: 'There existed no printed book bearing Gutenberg's name. Even today we know of only twenty-seven contemporary documents in which a Gutenberg was named, of which just twelve are extant, and only one mentions anything to do with printing.'[51] Johns argues that the cultural construction of printing was bolstered by the contemporary and historical hagiography of great men in the early years of European printing: Johannes Gutenberg, William Caxton, Aldus Manutius. Likewise, Hart was not the only person working on digitisation, but he was its most prominent and vocal advocate. Coupled with scant publicly available archival evidence of competing projects, just as with Gutenberg, Hart managed to bolster his claims of innovation. Both Hart and Gutenberg were entangled with a form of hagiography that strives to identify 'the first' when historical evidence instead points towards a slower, more diffuse move towards new technologies. While Gutenberg's canonisation largely occurred after his death, Hart actively encouraged this process once Project Gutenberg gained popularity in the early days of the Web.

In the latter half of the twentieth century, Johannes Gutenberg was appropriated as the patron saint of 'the information age', initially by Marshall McLuhan in his 1962 publication *The Gutenberg Galaxy*, which argues that the then emerging digital age would be as influential as the printing press in the fifteenth century. As the 'electronic age' coalesced into the early Web at the turn of the twenty-first century, McLuhan's ideas were

[49] Mullaney, *Chinese Typewriter*, 78.   [50] Kilgour, *Evolution of the Book*, 8.
[51] Johns, *Nature of the Book*, 329–30.

expanded further in the mass market futurism of *WIRED* magazine through its early editorial direction which exemplified what Fred Turner describes as a 'particular blend of libertarian politics, countercultural aesthetics, and techno-utopian visions' that Richard Barbrook and Andy Cameron called 'the "Californian Ideology"'.[52] Tom Petitt extends this argument by suggestion that the 'fixity' of the printing press (rebuked by book historical research) was part of the 'Gutenberg Parenthesis' where digital publishing marked a return to the greater fluidity of orality.[53] Hart diverges from this position but nonetheless, remained focused on the connection to Gutenberg. Since McLuhan-Silicon Valley boosterism was not assured to become the dominant form of computational thinking in the early 1970s, Hart's appropriation might have come to be the dominant narrative if the personal computer was not so successful. Despite this ideological grounding, Hart was not widely accepted into the Silicon Valley establishment but rather continued to influence at the margins during the 1990s. For example, he did not receive a profile in *WIRED*, the technological determinism bible during the 1990s, until 1997.[54]

His *WIRED* interview highlighted some of the reasons for the technology establishment's rejection of Project Gutenberg. Hart suggested the Project's mission was 'to get rid of the Trivial Pursuit aspect of education, and the monetary aspect of literature'.[55] His altruism stood in juxtaposition to the race to monetise the early Web. Once access had expanded from institutions to individuals, community projects were largely replaced by companies such as Amazon and eBay who radically transformed how people used the Web. It is telling that even in the early 2020s, Project Gutenberg remains advertisement-free other than a small unintrusive request for donations.

While he lacked the profit motive of other tech leaders, he nonetheless retained a form of digital colonialism embedded within similar projects such as Nicholas Negroponte's One Laptop One Child scheme: 'He foresees

[52] Turner, *From Counterculture to Cyberculture*.
[53] Pettitt, 'Before the Gutenberg Parenthesis'.
[54] Hamilton, 'Hart of the Gutenberg Galaxy'.
[55] Silberman, 'A Thousand Classics for the ASCIIng'.

the day when, armed with the trashiest laptop and a modem, tribesmen in Borneo's rain forest will be able to click onto Gutenberg and download texts.'[56] As with Negroponte's vision of cheap, repairable laptops solving the Global South's problems, Hart's desire to share free texts recalls earlier missionary movements in a deeply problematic manner, only exacerbated by the lack of diversity in curation when encouraging users to digitise their primary interests, leading to the reinforcement of the idea of the canon of white men, that I discuss further in Chapter 6.

Hart's sought to leverage his reputation within the Internet's standard folklore. In a letter sent to eminent Nobel Prize winners, he requested his nomination, suggesting his work on, and financing of, Project Gutenberg merited a Nobel Prize.[57] It is unclear why personally financing and administering a website is worthy of a Nobel Prize, especially since Hart was not the only one working on such a resource. Nonetheless, he wished to use the cultural capital of institutions such as the Nobel Prize to enshrine what he believed to be his long-term reputation, even in the face of overwhelming contradictory evidence. In other words, he believed that it was his right to claim the territory of digitisation.

3.2 Plain Text and Paratext

Compared to contemporary and later digitisation projects, Hart had a unique approach in terms of prioritising plain text over other forms of content presentation. Earlier projects often focused on text as searchable data via information retrieval.[58] Later, digitisers prioritised the fidelity of the page or introduced additional markup for semantic or presentational benefits. Meanwhile, Hart was a steadfast proponent of plain text, arguing that it was the most universal and accessible format. This led to jeremiads such as 'Graphics Versus ASCII', [American Standard Code for Information Interchange, a map of the Latin alphabet to binary code based on telegraph transmission], where Hart launched into a lengthy attack

---

[56] Hamilton, 'Hart of the Gutenberg Galaxy'; See Ames, *The Charisma Machine* for further details on the One Laptop One Child project.

[57] Hart, 'Prizes.Txt'.

[58] Bourne and Hahn, *History of Online Information Services*.

on bitmap representation that dominated the development of Adobe's PDF format.[59]

His firm belief in plain text publication had consequences for the books' paratexts, or the collection of 'secondary signals' that surround the main text including 'prefaces, postfaces, notices, forewords, etc; marginal, infrapaginal, terminal notes; epigraphs; illustrations; blurbs, book covers, [and] dust jackets'.[60] In Hart's vision, most of these elements should be removed to prioritise the main body. For example, ASCII has no typographic provision for bold or italicised text. Both the textual and physical materials have been stripped through this shift. It is also notable that initially this was accompanied by a lack of interest from Hart, with no available evidence of broader pushback, in reintroducing new paratext as the texts sat on a server without any cover image or any paratext beyond limited metadata for discoverability.

Despite Hart's early insistence on 'vanilla ASCII', the Project quickly diversified into other file formats. Most frequently, this would come in the form of a HTML edition of a long document or a file with lots of images, such as the illustrated editions of Lewis Carrol's *Alice in Wonderland*, but many older files also appeared in other formats that ran counter to Hart's ambitions. For example, the 1991 version of *Alice in Wonderland* was also available as a PDB (Palm Database), TeX, or PostScript file, three esoteric formats that required specialist knowledge to compile and use in the early 1990s.[61] There is no metadata noting when these files were uploaded, which leads to anachronisms such as PDB files which would be readable on a Palm Portable Digital Assistant (PDA), a portable computer and precursor to the smartphone, released in 1996. Some of the publication formats, including TeX and PostScript, were markup languages designed for printing rather than screen reading, although both can be rendered as PDFs. It is difficult to design a format simultaneously optimised for screen and print: a book's portrait orientation clashes with the landscape orientation of monitors; long-form text on a webpage often requires a dedicated print option to remove extraneous navigation elements. The choice to use TeX and

[59] Hart, 'Graphics Versus ASCII', *Bit.Listserv.Gutnberg*, 23 February 1993.
[60] Genette, *Palimpsests*, 3. [61] Carroll, *Alice's Adventures*.

PostScript intentionally prioritised print reuses above digital consumption. Conversely, including a PDB hints at a direction the Project would take once e-readers became more popular. While plain ASCII, optimised for reading on a screen with sixty characters per line in all capitals, is legible on a regular PC monitor, it is less than optimal for a small PDA or e-reader. The PDB would allow the text to be readable on a device not optimised for long-form reading. More recent publications have expanded upon this effort of including e-reader friendly versions as users can now choose between an EPUB or Kindle file. As consumption habits have changed to reading on-screen, Project Gutenberg adapted by calling publications 'e-books' instead of the more esoteric 'etexts'. Volunteers now create a HTML version as the original that can then be adapted into other file formats, including plain text, that users can download.

The only paratext that consistently appears with Project Gutenberg books is the lengthy front and back matter with requests and legal guidance. The front matter requests further help to reach an audience who might not already be engaged with the day-to-day running of the Project through the mailing lists and Usenet. In the first draft of Arthur Conan Doyle's *Beyond the City*, a rare text attributed to Hart in the 1990s, he asked for crowd-sourced proofreading: 'This book was particularly difficult to scan, due to age, type, and other factors. Your help in additional proofreading should be greatly appreciated. Thanks!'.[62] The self-reported publication dates are too unreliable to count as authoritative evidence, but at least one more edition was posted after the original before the renewal of all old Project Gutenberg content in the early 2000s, facilitated by the introduction of Distributed Proofreaders. A comparison of the two files shows that Hart did not receive extensive help with proofreading, but the largest and most frequent changes come from re-formatting the text from sixty to eighty characters per line. Nonetheless, these kinds of stubs encouraged new volunteers to engage with the Project with a low-stakes request rather than manually digitising something from scratch.

Despite Hart's insistence on plain text, he was not unfamiliar with textual scholarship and the importance of the materiality of text. His father, Hymen

---

[62] Conan Doyle, *Beyond the City*.

Hart, worked on cryptography in the Second World War before teaching
Shakespeare at Marshall University in West Virginia from 1972 to 1989,
rising to the rank of full professor in 1981.[63] Hymen's dissertation's title
indicates a clear focus on editorial matters: *Edward Capell: The First Modern
Editor of Shakespeare*.[64] Michael and Hymen even collaborated on the
abandoned Shakespeare digitisation project during the 1980s.[65] Hart
acknowledged the influence of his father in a newsletter on the anniversary
of his death, advertising the release of Sebastian Evans's *The High History of
the Holy Graal*.[66] Hart cannot claim that he was ignorant of nuances of
textual scholarship and the importance of the material document, but he
persisted with his belief in what Daniel Pargman and Jacob Palme term
'ASCII imperialism' even when the technical conditions were no longer an
issue.[67]

   There was clearer evidence of Hart's appreciation of the nuances of
textual scholarship in his notes for the US Constitution:

> The following edition of The Constitution of the United
> States of America has been based on many hours of study of
> a variety of editions, and will include certain variant spel-
> lings, punctuation, and capitalization as we have been able to
> reasonable ascertain belonged to the original. In case of
> internal discrepancies in these matters, most or all have
> been left.[68]

While Hart was keen to emphasise the fluidity of the central document of
US law, this did not extend to a lot of other texts where there is little-to-no
information on its provenance which can only be reconstructed through
external materials or through the work of conscientious digitisers included

[63] Office of University Relations, 'Memorial Service to Honor Hymen', 2; Office of
     University Relations, 'Promotion and Tenure', 1.
[64] Hymen Hart, 'Edward Capell'. [65] Murphy, *Shakespeare in Print*, 333.
[66] Hart and Humanist Discussion Group, '10.0519 Gutenberg Project Newsletter'.
[67] Pargman and Palme, 'ASCII Imperialism'.
[68] Founding Fathers, 'The United States' Constitution'.

at least the year and publisher in the final files. This was an inevitable consequence of the attempt to prioritise plain text over everything else. Hart's insistence on just including the main text made it difficult to detect provenance or gain a more nuanced understanding of the text's transmission history.

Despite occasional posting non-ASCII files, the Project never became a beacon for the community working on e-books designed for early portable digital reading including the Game Boy and PDAs.[69] This was despite volunteers offering pre-formatted files. For example, in 1993, Harry Chesley asked Hart if he would be interested in hosting Newton (Apple's early PDA) readable versions on the server.[70] There is no response in Hart's archived emails and no evidence that these files were ever posted. While Hart initially targeted academics, his fights with the TEI community and the OTA, discussed in the next section, narrowed the potential for expansion. Instead, by 2005, in an interview with Sam Vaknin, Hart noted 'our target audience is the person on the street, not the ivy tower scholars, who all want to take over how our books should look'.[71] His approach reveals a broader shift in sharing texts online between the 1990s and 2000s. Initially these texts would primarily be circulated for data analysis but as computers became more mobile there was an increasing demand for accessible marked-up versions of the text. Hart yearned for the former and only reluctantly began to include the latter after amateur communities developed elsewhere.

3.3 The Dangers of the Lone Genius Myth

The mythology behind Michael Hart helped bolster the reputation of Project Gutenberg in the long run, but at times in the 1980s and 1990s when the Project began to grow, he was a liability. Hart enjoyed participating in academic mailing lists and would frequently fall into flame wars about contentious issues. Humanist was highly active at this time with considerable excitement around new initiatives including the Text Encoding Initiative (TEI), a spinoff of Standardised General Markup Language

---

[69] 'GameBoy Books to Go'.

[70] Harry Chesley to Michael Hart, 'Network readable versions', 18 November 1993.

[71] Vaknin, 'The Ubiquitous Project Gutenberg'.

(SGML) designed to allow more sophisticated computational analysis than plain text formatting. The Oxford Text Archive were keen proponents of TEI, which led to a long-standing public feud between Hart and members of the OTA/TEI community including most prominently, Lou Burnard. This debate revolved around the importance of marked-up text, favoured by academics, and the vanilla ASCII prevalent in early Project Gutenberg publications. SGML was used for both structural (how should this text look when printed/rendered on the screen) and semantic (for example, marking up poetry or edits that occurred in earlier versions of the text) markup, ensuring it had a broad userbase. Burnard was a strong proponent of the revolutionary potential of markup, writing to Humanist in 1989: 'Dare I mention that the answer to all the technical problems would be the widespread acceptance of SGML without the publishing industry? Then all we'd have to worry about would be the copyright problems.'[72] Burnard's optimism for the benefits of markup ran against broader currents within trade publishing where digital innovation was treated with suspicion even after the arrival of the Kindle in 2007.

Hart spent much of the early 1990s attacking the OTA and TEI. His belief in the supremacy of plain text stymied the greater acceptance of the Project as it presented technical challenges for those unfamiliar with reading plain text, especially once computing processing and storage costs dropped sufficiently to remove the technical limitations that guided Hart's initial decision. This approach to text encoding came with challenges, especially with the early limitations of screen technologies. When explaining why a lot of the early digitisations had to be corrected, Hart explained:

> I know that at my own Xerox Sigma V, we had a very limited [character] set that did not include lower case or many punctuation marks, and so I have made it clear in the modern files that I rewrote them in lower case at a much later date.[73]

[72] Lou Burnard to Humanist Discussion Group, '3.270: Why Publishers' May Be of Little Use', 20 July 1989.
[73] Michael S. Hart to Book People mailing list, !'!@[Redacted] Re: !@[Redacted] Re: Early Ebook History Info Wanted; "Alice"'. 13 January 2006.

Early evidence suggests that Hart was initially interested in machine readability, and he only started to consider human consumption at a later date once he understood the benefits. For example, in 1989 Hart advertised PG as part of the University of Illinois Personal Computer User Group's Machine Readable Classics Special Interest Group.[74] It is only with the later acknowledgement of reading on screen and the rise of early forms of the e-book that Hart makes the shift from text to book surrogate and correspondingly shaping the Project around a new ideal.

Hart drew the ire of this community partially from his early framing of the Project. Bob Kraft asked Hart a series of questions around how Project Gutenberg interacted with 'related endeavors at a wide variety of levels', its funding mechanisms, and if it 'also want[s] English language material that are not among the 10,000 most used books'.[75] He continued that 'there is clearly a "missionary" aspect to the Project – to get people informed and involved' but asked how it fit in to the broader infrastructure?[76] As in this case, Hart's selective interactions with other similar projects, often to boost the profile of PG rather than a truly collaborative effort, led to a distrust from third parties. The feud simmered for three years on Humanist with Burnard deriding events Hart was invited to speak at.[77] Hart panicked at the level of pushback he received, posting: 'I think we are going to need a volunteer to assist in the area of Public Relations [in the wake of flame wars].'[78]

In terms of their ideological differences, both were proven wrong with the emergence of the Portable Document Format (PDF) as the preferred method for long-form reading on screen for many years and the ascent of HTML on the Web at the expense of semantically rich Extensible Mark-up Language (XML) schema such as TEI. Once screens were able to render

---

[74] Hart, 'More Shakespeare', 6–7.

[75] Bob Kraft to Humanist Discussion Group, '3.301 M.S. Hart on e-Texts', 28 July 1989.

[76] Bob Kraft to Humanist Discussion Group, 'Project Gutenberg', 10 May 1990.

[77] Lou Burnard to Humanist Discussion Group, '5.0949: Hart at Neach', 22 April 1992.

[78] Hart, 'Volunteer Need for PR', *Bit.Listserv.Gutnberg*, 13 April 1992. Emphasis mine.

bitmap images rather than offering basic terminal interfaces, plain text was
no longer the most appropriate choice for consuming text on a screen.
Additionally, SGML and TEI are difficult formats to learn and use due to
their structural and semantic complexity. HTML simplified SGML so that
non-technical users could make attractive webpages, especially once the
infrastructural tools were more advanced. Meanwhile PDF offered an easy-
to-create print facsimile that became the default for much on-screen reading
whatever the drawbacks. These other tools would disappear into the background to become part of workflows to produce texts rather than central to
their dissemination and consumption.

By February 1992, Hart posted an email entitled 'Apology' to
HUMANST. In the email, he specifically mentions prominent figures in
the TEI community and notes that 'I am not trying to change the
scholarly, the intellectual or any of the other groups I have referenced
as being "anti." I just want to put out books of no more than reasonable
quality for a general audience'.[79] Nonetheless, even by 1996, Hart was still
reciting these common talking points: 'The major factors of these messages are that I join their causes, in some virtual conspiracy to promote
their favorite markup schemes.'[80] In an undated mid-2000s script for
a speech, Hart still dwelled on the arguments: '*1990's ~ Oxford U tries to
take over the world of eBooks, fails.*'[81] Vanilla ASCII texts were never
optimised for ease of reading, and as the Project scaled, the average user
did not have the technical ability to convert the ASCII into a more
readable format. E-reader-friendly versions of Gutenberg texts enabled
a new audience to read these works. The external threat of paid versions of
the texts being available directly with the Kindle and other e-book stores
pushed this shift in focus. This was a clear incentive for PG to ensure users
had a frictionless experience that would demonstrate how Hart's ideological preferences could be supplanted by the necessity to adopt to new
standards.

---

[79]   Michael S. Hart to Project Gutenberg Email List, 'Apology', 29 February 1992.
[80]   Michael Hart, 'Message From Michael Hart About Flames', *Bit.Listserv.Gutnberg*,
       31 July 1996.
[81]   Hart, 'Mt.Specifics.Txt'.

3.4 Conclusion

Hart clearly believed that Project Gutenberg was an empty vessel to push his broader ideological concerns around digital reading and technology more broadly. Nonetheless, he would often undermine his own ideological principles in practice even if he thoroughly defended his position in online debates. Just as with his hagiography, we can begin to revise this view of Project Gutenberg if we move towards a 'zeitgeist' model of digitisation history where collaboration is more important than individual geniuses or polymaths. In order to grow beyond multiple individual projects in silos, it is important to develop a communal infrastructure that enables further team work. This requires a greater degree of organisation that we can see Project Gutenberg achieved through both technological and social means in what can be termed its *platformisation*. Through tracing the increased platformisation of Project Gutenberg, we can begin to move from a heroic to a sociological historiography of the Project.

4 Technological Platforms

In the digital age, we need to consider not just the people in the narrative, but also the technology enabling their work. In the second half of this Element, I will explore the importance of technical and political platforms to the development of Project Gutenberg. This follows a rupture in the scholarship around platforms in the early 2010s between those interested in 'platform architecture' as canvas for computational creativity steered by Nick Montfort and Ian Bogost's *Racing the Beam* and subsequent steward-ship of the Platform Studies book series, and the 'political turn' in digital media studies around social media platforms such as Facebook.[82] As I have argued elsewhere, these two bodies of scholarship are linked as the social and the technical are inseparable in real world uses of these platforms.[83] Nonetheless, I follow this disciplinary split in order to first, in this chapter, demonstrate the importance of mature technological infrastructure to the Project's success in the 1990s, and, then in the next chapter, explore how platform governance solidified this progress while simultaneously hindering efforts to rapidly increase the quantity of material available via PG.

Until the late 1980s, Project Gutenberg was largely a solo endeavour for Michael Hart. The Project remained dormant during this time, at least from the public perspective, but by the early 1990s, conditions were ripe for PG's growth. While only 2,000 computers had Internet access in 1985, almost 160,000 devices were connected in 1989.[84] Many of these computers were still housed in universities, but more users were able to access the machines. With this growth, more people would be interested in Hart's mission and would be willing to volunteer. The year 1989 was also the year Tim Berners-Lee conceptualised the World Wide Web as a protocol to enable more effective textual transmission at European Organization for Nuclear Research (CERN) before its public launch in January 1991. The Web further accelerated the number of users on the Internet, ensuring a rapidly growing demand and volunteer base. It is no coincidence that the re-emergence of Project Gutenberg began in 1989 and Hart's site had become

---

[82] Montfort and Bogost, *Racing the Beam*; Gillespie, 'The Politics of "Platforms"'.

[83] Rowberry, *Four Shades of Gray*. [84] Abbate, *Inventing the Internet*, 186.

established in the popular imagination by the mid-1990s when more users were coming online, albeit through disjointed channels. In this chapter, I trace the re-emergence of Project Gutenberg in the early years of the Web to assess how Hart used this new platform and a rapidly growing audience to solidify PG's position as the most well-known digitisation project. This reputation also allowed Hart to access and share more advanced equipment for digitising.

The importance of technology to the Project can be illustrated by how Hart made use of other institutions' resources. Project Gutenberg relied on university servers for web hosting to bring down costs. Hart was also a successful fundraiser for the organisation, often receiving hardware and service support from various large technology companies:

> Hart doesn't need high-end stuff to run Gutenberg – it's just nice to have around. Every few years, he gets a computer from Apple, NeXt, IBM, or Hewlett-Packard. Bell & Howell once donated a $50,000 scanner, to help volunteers input books quickly. And he's thinking about setting up an email server, so he can offer free accounts to Gutenberg volunteers. Just talking about the idea gets him giggling with glee.[85]

While he downplayed the significance of this equipment, the metadata from early Gutenberg books show how vital it was in encouraging others to digitise material.

4.1 Building Communities Online

In 1989, it was not clear that the Web would come to dominate the way we interacted online. Use of the Internet could broadly be split in two: (1) social interaction; and (2) file transfers. Before the Web's public launch, various rival platforms vied for the same audience in both fields before the Web began to be the standard location for both. Discourse around Web 2.0 and the Social Web suggests that the Web was not social prior to the early 2000s,

---

[85] Hamilton, 'Hart of the Gutenberg Galaxy'.

but that does not mean that people were not communicating over the Internet. While there were many protocols and systems (including most prominently email), Usenet and mailing lists were both early points of social interaction at a broadcast level that remained an important part of the Internet's social infrastructure, even beyond the emergence of Web 2.0.

4.1.1 Usenet and Mailing Lists

Usenet had been a vital part of early Internet communication since 1979. It was 'a distributed discussion system built on a decentralised network of servers ferrying user messages to subscribers across the network. The network was restructured in 1987 (known colloquially as the Great Renaming), around eight "official" hierarchies, known as the Big 8: comp.*, misc.*, news.*, rec.*, sci.*, soc.*, humanities.* and talk*'.[86] Decentralisation was part of the core appeal of the platform as it allowed users to create their own niche sublists according to specific interests. Dame-Griff recounts that Usenet had a complex infrastructure that required a level of technical expertise: 'As a distributed network, users had many different access points to Usenet. Long-time users, particularly prior to 1993, primarily used newsreaders, specialised software that included now-familiar affordances like message threading, marking messages as read, and message quoting, as well as Usenet-specific filtering tools, like killfiles.'[87] Due to these technical requirements, the general audience of Usenet had a high level of technical literacy, which was useful for Hart's initial goals of cultivating an audience able to digitise public domain materials, if not for broader consumption.

Despite these challenges, Usenet became a prominent proto-social network due to user's abilities to create their own alt.* groups that were easily discoverable. For example, rec.arts.tv is a group dedicated towards any topics related to television shows. These lists were free to join with minimal moderation. bit.listserv.gutnberg and www-talk were two popular communities that Hart either created or frequented and both became popular due to the rise of the Web and the potential for users to shape the policy of Project

---

[86] Dame-Griff, 'Herding the "Performing Elephants"'.
[87] Dame-Griff, 'Herding the "Performing Elephants"'.

Gutenberg and the Web respectively. Before the widespread adoption of mailing lists (discussed below), Usenet was a useful broadcast tool, especially for users who did not have access to the relevant email addresses of individuals who might be interested.

If Usenet required some technical skill to access, mailing lists transformed the more common email protocol into a broadcast medium. Mailing lists proliferated in the late 1980s in response to new tools such as Bitnet, which was a prominent piece of infrastructure designed as a 'technical cooperative to establish a network among [East Coast] universities that had computing centers with IBM mainframes'.[88] After an initial period of funding from IBM between 1981 and 1987, Bitnet had to make a transition towards other revenue streams. Their solution was to create Listserv, a software package that facilitated email mailing lists, and charging membership fees for other institutions to use the software. Listserv quickly became the preference for cross-institutional collaborations and online community building as it was easy to set up as it worked entirely over the established email protocol, while also providing an archive.[89]

Usenet and mailing lists encouraged several collaborators beyond Hart's immediate social circle to join. Alongside this, he had attended various conferences in the late 1980s and early 1990s, including the American Library Association, the American Society for Cybernetics, and the Institute for Graphic Communication. After these events, he had built up several contacts within academic and library communities in North America rather than the broader community that he could find via the Web, Usenet, and mailing lists. Hart successfully used mailing lists to recruit specialist volunteers. For example, in September 1992, he sent out a 'CALL FOR WIZARDS AND GURUS' looking for someone who would be able to help with a recently acquired NeXT machine.[90] Likewise, Hart would frequently receive unsolicited digitisations through both his private email

---

[88] Grier and Campbell, 'Social History of Bitnet', 33.

[89] Grier and Campbell, 34–5.

[90] Michael S. Hart, 'Call for Wizards and Gurus', *Bit.Listserv.Gutnberg*, 3 September 1992.

and the Project Gutenberg listserv.[91] Volunteers would write 'I am willing to do just about anything to help. I would love to work with you to design/host an advertising-supported PG Web/FTP site on BookWire'.[92] Through building the reputation of the Project via early social media, Hart assembled a larger group of volunteers than he could have reached through face-to-face networking.

4.1.2 FTP and Gopher

Online social platforms formed the cornerstone of early collaborations alongside regular mail, but uploading the final product remained a second obstacle given the infrastructure of the early Internet. There were two main competitors to the Web in the early 1990s: File Transfer Protocol (FTP) and Gopher. FTP is the oldest of the three protocols, dating back to April 1971 with Abhay K. Bhushan's Request for Comments (RFC) 114.[93] This early implementation places it before many of the modern elements of the Internet such as Transmission Control Protocol/Internet Protocol (TCP/IP), the main mechanism for transmitting data across a distributed network. FTP was therefore an established protocol in the late 1980s but one that made discoverability difficult as each directory had to be manually indexed. It was not the only way to transfer data but it became one of the more established mechanisms. FTP's permission system offered granular read-write access while HTTP was read-only. This access could be personalised for individual accounts so a few administrators had full read-write access, while others could just access content.

Early PG files include instructions for how to access the files through a command line:

```
ftp sunsite.unc.edulogin: anonymous
password: your@login
cd pub/docs/books/gutenberg
cd etext90 through etext99
dir [to see files]
```

---

[91] K. McMahon, 'Text Offer to Project Gutenberg', *Bit.Listserv.Gutnberg*, 21 September 1992.

[92] Jamey Bennett to John Chua, 'Re: Re: Hello', 27 July 1995.

[93] Bhushan, 'RFC 114'.

get or mget [to get files. . .set bin for zip files]
GET GUTINDEX.?? [to get a year's listing of books, e.g., GUTINDEX.99]
GET GUTINDEX.ALL [to get a listing of ALL books][94]

These step-by-step instructions guided users through the process of locating the FTP server, finding materials, and downloading them. While some of the commands contain comments in square brackets, there is an expectation that users will understand that 'cd' stands for 'change directory' or that they should use 'get' to download one file and 'mget' to download more than one file. Furthermore, the index files that provide greater context for where users might find the material most relevant to them are only mentioned at the end of the instructions. The tutorial is therefore aimed at proficient Internet users as it is unlikely that everyone would understand how to use the command line, especially as this boilerplate was attached to e-books published as late as 1999 when Web use was mainstream. While it is possible for servers to act as sites for both upload and download, the upload server was separate from downloads: mrcnext.cso.uiuc.edu. This ensured users were not mistakenly provided incorrect permissions or upload publicly available material that had not been fully checked for copyright infringement. As the domain name denotes, this upload server was located on the University of Illinois's Computer Science servers from the Project's early years.

FTP remained a versatile upload protocol especially after the rise of the Web. 'Browsing the Web', as the name indicates, was a read-only process where users could access a page that had been separately uploaded. FTP was one of the more common ways of making updates to remote servers displaying Web content. Consequently, it remained a popular method of transferring files, especially larger ones, between individuals in lieu of the now-familiar 'cloud computing' services. Due to its early integration into Project Gutenberg workflows, it became the dominant storage site for completed and work-in-progress texts. As a complete read-write protocol with sufficiently advanced permissions systems, it also doubled up as a useful mechanism for allowing users to access publications.

---

[94] Project Gutenberg, ed., *King James Bible*.

If FTP was the established method of transferring files online, Gopher represented the new competition to the Web, having been created at the University of Minnesota's Microcomputer Center in 1991 and turned into a IETF Request for Comments in March 1993.[95] Gopher was built on the same infrastructure as the Web, relying on 'a client-server model' where 'users run client software on their desktop systems, connecting to a server and sending the server a selector [...] via a TCP connection at a well-known port'.[96] Ultimately, the Web was the most successful platform as it was a more versatile and responsive standard, including hypertext. Gopher still persists in a hobbyist community – in fact, PG continued to maintain a presence on Gopher until summer 1995 – and FTP retained a community especially within illegal file sharing communities, although in recent years Web browsers have stopped offering access to FTP servers directly within their interface. As early Web standards emphasised documents over multimedia, or even images in the first implementation, it was the natural home for Project Gutenberg.[97]

4.1.3 The World Wide Web

The origins of the Web are well recounted as one of the technological landmarks of the last fifty years, but it is worth pausing to consider why the Web was so successful compared to other protocols.[98] While other protocols (FTP, Gopher) focused on file transfer, Tim Berners-Lee, the inventor of the Web, developed the system for document sharing and viewing at CERN. This led to the design decision to split the mechanism for content delivery (Hypertext Transfer Protocol or HTTP) and how to render those texts (Hypertext Markup Language or HTML). Berners-Lee addressed an important aspect of discoverability with the development of HTTP through the creation of 'the uniform resource locator (URL) – a standard address format that specifies both the type of application protocol being used and the address of the computer that has the desired data'.[99] URLs were service

---

[95]   McCahill et al., 'RFC 1436'.   [96]   McCahill et al., 'RFC 1436'.
[97]   'Tags Used in HTML'.
[98]   See Berners-Lee, *Weaving the Web* for an authoritative account of the Web's origin story.
[99]   Abbate, *Inventing the Internet*, 215.

agnostic, allowing users to have a standardised form for accessing FTP, Usenet, Gopher, email, and Web-based content using a single format, thus lowering the skill barrier to access these various protocols.[100]

HTML, the second pillar of the Web, was also a transformative use of a pre-existing technology that improved its accessibility. Berners-Lee modified SGML, itself a descendent of IBM's General Markup Language, an early digital typesetting system that publishers had been using since what John Maxwell terms the 'Early Digital' period of the 1970s.[101] Trade publishers were slow to use SGML in their production workflows because of the steep learning curve and the requirement for users to develop their own set of tags and publish these standards. This benefitted users who wished to customise materials but would be difficult to maintain for users who might be accessing the same content on different web browsers which might not be able to correctly interpret unknown tags. HTML took the idea and created a small number of tags to structure a document that was universal across different implementations (although this soon became an issue with the so-called 'browser wars' as different browsers elected to introduce unique tags).

Berners-Lee wanted to encourage Hart to publish PG on the Web as seen from discussions on the www-talk mailing list:

> One possibility is we feed back the hypertext to Michael Hart. It could just be an overlay of files which have pointers to the actual text, or a smart server which can #include the actual text into a wrapper document.
>
> Nat, do you think the Gutenberg project would consider using their existing distribution chain for the stuff? We could set up W3 servers on some of their machines maybe? It would take less CPU than FTP.[102]

Hart rejected Berners-Lee's overtures to use HTML, but he was keen to distribute publications over HTTP rather than the more complex

---

[100] Abbate, *Inventing the Internet*, 215. [101] Maxwell, 'Coach House Press'.

[102] Tim Berners-Lee to www-talk, 'Re: Project Gutenberg's Roget's Thesaurus', 13 April 1993.

read-write system of FTP. Moving away from more difficult protocols such as FTP and Gopher would allow the Project to grow its audience, and consequentially volunteer base, to a level that had not previously been possible. This came at a loss of direct interaction and read-write interfaces within the primary sites, but, nonetheless, the rapid uptake of users on the Web was an opportunity for Hart to grow the platform.

As the Web began to mature and gather audiences from various other protocols, Hart had an opportunity to re-orient the Project. As part of this re-emergence, PG released the first five 'e-texts' in November 1993 to celebrate 'the 230th anniversary of The Gettysburg Address, and the 30th anniversary of the assassination of John Fitzgerald Kennedy: also in anticipation of the release of Project Gutenberg Etext #100'.[103] This also allowed for the texts to be updated for a new audience. This reframing would not make use of the affordances of HTML, but it would move away from the terminal-driven all caps format of those early releases in their original context. This was the start of a constant update cycle for older texts without a complete level of version control to ensure that records of the earlier versions remained for posterity. Despite moving to the Web, Hart was deeply sceptical it was an advance on previous protocols, with Denise Hamilton noting that 'he considers the Web an appalling waste of bandwidth – Gutenberg's main files reside on an FTP site' as part of Hart's 1997 *WIRED* profile.[104]

4.2 Digitisation Equipment

As the demand for human and machine-readable texts increased, Hart needed to move away from manual to automated methods of digitisation. In October 1990, Hart applied for an equipment loan from Apple Computers through the company's Apple Library of Tomorrow (A LOT) scheme, spearheaded by Monica Ertel, Apple's Corporate Librarian.[105] Apple devised

[103] Michael S. Hart, 'Early Project Gutenberg Etext', *Bit.Listserv.Gutnberg*, 15 November 1993.

[104] Hamilton, 'Hart of the Gutenberg Galaxy'.

[105] Michael Hart to Monica Ertel, 'Request for Mac and Scanner [Bitmail]', 22 October 1990, Series 4 Box 6 Folder 21, Apple Computer Inc Records 1977–1997 Corporate Library Misc Files; Steve Cisler to Kathy Askew, 'New Order

A LOT to work with library initiatives on digitisation projects which Hart saw as an opportunity to get some extra equipment. He successfully bid for a loan of Mac equipment including a Mac IIci, a portrait display, and an Apple Scanner.[106] Simultaneously, Hart was in the market for equipment from Steve Jobs's second computer company, NeXT, soliciting the company for equipment in 1992.[107] Through both mailing list posts and the acknowledgements in early versions of publications, we can see additional references to Caere, IBM, and many other companies who lent equipment to advance the Project's goals. Once again, Hart's ability as a prominent networker ensured his collaborators did not have to type everything manually.

Ilana and Greg Newby made use of the Apple equipment in their October 1992 digitisation of Washington Irving's *The Legend of Sleepy Hollow* suggesting that the equipment was kept local but available for others.[108] By the end of 1993, another round of equipment was passed on to other prominent collaborators outside of Illinois. For example, in December 1993 Judy Boss ramped up her digitisation efforts. The colophon for Edgar Rice Burrough's *Tarzan and the Jewels of Opar* (#92) detailed her equipment including donations from Calera Recognition Systems, an Optical Character Recognition (OCR) developer, on an IBM computer with a Hewlett-Packard scanner[109] Likewise, by March 1994, Caere Corporation, the company behind OmniPage, had donated several copies of its software to volunteers who went on to become prominent digitisers, including John Hamm. An unattributed digitisation of George Eliot's *Middlemarch*, likely the work of Hart himself, includes mention of another copy of OmniPage Professional donated by Caere Corporation noting to contact Mike Lough at the company for further information.[110] The extant evidence suggests that these volunteers only became power users after receiving this equipment. Nonetheless, from that point onwards it became common practice to see information about scanning from both those who

---

[Project Gutenberg]', 19 November 1990, Series 4 Box 6 Folder 21, Apple Computer Inc Records 1977–1997 Corporate Library Misc Files.

[106] Cisler to Askew, 'New Order [Project Gutenberg]', 19 November 1990.

[107] Hart, 'Call for Wizards and Gurus'. [108] Irving, *Legend of Sleepy Hollow*.

[109] Burroughs, *Tarzan and the Jewel of Opar*. [110] Eliot, *Middlemarch*.

received free equipment and those who otherwise had access. The equipment available to the Project's collaborators was instrumental in accelerating its growth, albeit at the cost of smaller contributions.

4.3 Conclusion

Hart was not solely responsible for the lack of traction with Project Gutenberg prior to the emergence of the Web in the early 1990s. It is difficult to cultivate an audience if you are an early adopter. Once the infrastructure and user base began to grow with the coalescence of various technologies including the Web, Usenet, and mailing lists, Hart was well poised to ensure that Project Gutenberg could thrive under these conditions. Production doubled almost every year over the mid-1990s as he leveraged this network. The Web's technical infrastructure also offered new opportunities for Hart to consider what sort of a repository he wanted to develop. This led to experimentation with other file formats although this was limited by the bandwidth of many users at the time. This technical infrastructure was essential for ensuring that more users could both produce and access content, but this needed to be matched by a higher level of platform governance to ensure that PG could continue to grow throughout the 1990s.

5 Platform Governance

The technical infrastructure for the Web was undeniably important for the formation of Project Gutenberg, but we cannot ignore the social and legal factors driving the rise of platforms. The framing of social media companies, including Facebook and YouTube, as 'platforms' emerged from their rhetorical distancing from the term 'publisher', thereby reducing their liability for the user-generated content uploaded to their servers and transforming the terms of their relationship with content creators and their audiences. Using the example of YouTube, Tarleton Gillespie argues, the term 'platform' allows companies 'to make a broadly progressive sales pitch while also eliding the tensions inherent in [their services]: between user-generated and commercially-produced content, between cultivating community and serving up advertising'.[111]

In the wake of scandals such as Facebook's partnership with Cambridge Analytica to siphon masses of data for political campaigns, there has been an increased interest in platform governance, or what Robert Gorwa calls the 'power dynamics and the effects of external political forces on the platform ecosystem'.[112] This work has led to exposés such as Sarah Roberts's *Behind the Screen* that focuses on the traumatising manual labour of content moderation on platforms like Facebook.[113] Project Gutenberg elides many of the more contentious issues of platform governance due to its small scale and policies of extensive content moderation. Nonetheless, how the Project engages with sociolegal challenges is vital to understand how it solidified its reputation as the primary community book digitisation platform in the era discussed in this book.

5.1 Funding Project Gutenberg

Hart oscillated between complaining about funding the whole Project himself or mentioning the 'various academic institutions and even some Texas oil interests [that] have offered to bankroll Gutenberg over the years,

---

[111] Gillespie, 'Politics of "Platforms"', 348.
[112] Gorwa, 'What Is Platform Governance?', 855.
[113] Roberts, *Beyond the Screen*.

in exchange for control. One university offered him a six-figure salary, he says, to bring the project to their campus. He turned them all down flat'.[114] The truth is somewhere between these two extremes. Labour is often the most expensive cost for a start-up but the majority of early PGers were volunteers. In 2001, Hart claimed 'other than ONE assistant to our Project Gutenberg Literary Archive Foundation trustee, Project Gutenberg has never had ANY paid people'.[115] Until the formation of the PGLAF, Hart's financial responsibility for the Project ensured that he retained the power and autonomy to shape the future strategic direction of the site.

Nonetheless, Hart was keen on exploiting institutional prestige with the Project. In its early years, he was able to leverage the connection to the University of Illinois, but this was unsustainable. In 1991, he outlined a ten-year exit strategy where he would give away 10 per cent of the Project each year to a different college before his retirement in 2011. He hoped that having ten invested institutions would improve the resilience of the Project.[116] In retrospect, these ambitions were never fulfilled and Hart would continue to lead Project Gutenberg up until his death in 2014, but there were some minor successes. Most prominently, Hart was able to pick up a salary as Professor of Electronic Text and sponsorship from Illinois Benedictine College who took over 10 per cent of the Project between 1991 and 2000.[117]

Hart listed other targets in late 1991, mentioning St John's College in Maryland and Carnegie-Mellon University (CMU) in Pittsburgh.[118] A deal never emerged with St John's, but Hart managed to find an institutional home at Carnegie-Mellon from 1997 to 2001. Both choices had significant symbolic capital for Hart. St John's College is known as the 'Great Books College', where students do not choose degree programmes but rather

---

[114] Hamilton, 'Hart of the Gutenberg Galaxy'.

[115] Michael S. Hart to Book People mailing list, 'Re: Sustaining on-Line Book Sites (Re: Named Word and Copyright)', 3 May 2001.

[116] Michael S. Hart, 'A Personal Note', *Bit.Listserv.Gutnberg*, 25 December 1991.

[117] Michael S. Hart, 'January 1992 Newsletter', *Bit.Listserv.Gutnberg*, 19 January 1992.

[118] Hart, 'A Personal Note'.

follow a set curriculum that focuses on canonical texts which are often in the public domain. The college's approach could clearly become a focus for the Project as it could offer the reading list for free online. Carnegie-Mellon was an equally symbolic choice: Andrew Carnegie, robber baron and philanthropist, founded the university along with several thousand libraries. Consequently, his name has become synonymous with literacy. CMU had also developed a reputation for engineering and humanities computing that would provide relevant support for Hart's activities. When this complete institutional support never emerged by Hart's self-imposed deadline of 2001, Greg Newby collaborated with Hart to create the Project Gutenberg Literary Archive Foundation (PGLAF), which remains the primary mechanism for administration to date.

5.2 Content Moderation

Hart and Newby's document 'Principles of Minimal Regulation/ Administration' offers an insight into how they viewed their administrative principles: 'the best thing Project Gutenberg can do to achieve the mission is often to simply get out of the way and let our volunteers do what they like best, and then help them make any adjustments that might be necessary to get their work to the most readers'.[119] This philosophical position runs counter to the Project's maximalist approach to content moderation that underpins much of the platform's governance. In short, after a string of unsuccessful attempts to upload material, usually still protected by copyright, Hart was keen to strictly monitor all proposed material and filter out anything that was likely to cause legal problems within the United States. The geographic limiter is important as PG have often chosen to block access to their publications in countries in legal dispute, choosing to argue that they only abide by US law. This has led to a series of 'cease and desist' lawsuits from Australia, Germany, and France.[120] As a consequence, PG has 'georestricted' some or all content in affected regions. The 'Principles of Minimal Regulation' cannot exist in isolation of the sociolegal reality of publishing material on the Internet.

---

[119] Hart and Newby, 'Minimal Regulation'.
[120] PGLAF, 'Cease and Desist Responses'.

In order to mitigate these external factors, Project Gutenberg deployed an early intervention system of content moderation whereby all publications receive several layers of scrutiny pre-publication to ensure they cause a minimal amount of issues. We can see this process as the reverse of the more popular approach of social media codified in Section 230, where service providers and platforms are not directly responsible for the content posted on their servers, with an obligation only to take content down once notified. It even runs counter to the attitude of Amazon and Google Books' approach to digitisation in the early 2000s where both companies digitised as much content as possible before dealing with the consequences. Project Gutenberg's response to takedown notices and pre-publication indicates a cautious approach to platform governance that can be traced back to the necessity to professionalise the Project after the relaunch in 1989.

5.3 Professionalisation and Governance

An increasing emphasis on professionalisation was vital for the sustainability of Project Gutenberg. Hart quickly realised that this was not a solo project and that he needed real expertise in specific areas if the Project was going to grow and adapt to the rapidly changing digital landscape. This went beyond expertise in copyright to considering how to consolidate and improve workflows. For example, by the mid-1990s Project Gutenberg was well organised for undertaking larger projects through automated means. In a request for a C programmer, Hart revealed that 'Project Gutenberg's volunteers have developed an OCR program specially designed to do the 25,000 pages of our upcoming encyclopedia'.[121] The final output was a copy of the 1911 edition of *Encyclopaedia Britannica*, one of the few larger digitisations undertaken in house by PG prior to 2000. Hiring more skilled developers also ensured Hart could scale the Project through automating work that had been painstakingly undertaken by individuals and small groups up to that point.

In the early 1990s, Hart actively recruited volunteers to take core administrative duties and he would assume an executive role although he 'never wanted to be any kind of executive or administrator, and if anyone

---

[121] Michael S. Hart, 'C Programmer Wanted', *Bit.Listserv.Gutnberg*, 31 July 1994.

would like to have an inside track at all or part of this job, please let [him] know'.[122] This followed another plea: 'Anyone who really wants to take over a large portion of Project Gutenberg's overall operation is more than encouraged to do so, or even small parts.'[123] This tension between controlling the narrative about the Project and Hart's importance on one hand and the increasing administrative burden of managing a growing community on the other became the defining characteristic of Project Gutenberg during the 1990s.

Hart built a core team of volunteers who were largely drawn from academic institutions in North America. The majority worked within library settings and provided a wide range of skills. For example in 1993, Mary Brandt Jensen, the Director of the University of San Diego Law Library, acted as Copyright Analyst for the Project in the early years including copyright clearance.[124] Other early contributors included Nathan Torkington (Victoria University of Wellington) and Geof Pawlicki (Stanford), who were both identified as 'Associate Directors', as well as Judy Boss and Marvin Peterson from the University of North Omaha who fulfilled the roles of type and proof partners.[125] Judy Boss would be particularly instrumental in the early years, with Hart awarding her a 'Certificate of Appreciation' in 1991, noting she was likely to also receive one in 1992.[126] By May 1997, Dianne Bean had joined the executive committee as the Director of Production, coordinating the distribution of scanning equipment and other aspects of getting texts online.[127] Through

---

[122] Michael S. Hart, 'Project Gutenberg Feb Newsletter', *Bit.Listserv.Gutnberg*, 2 February 1992.

[123] Michael S. Hart, 'PS', *Bit.Listserv.Gutnberg*, 28 February 1992.

[124] Michael S. Hart, 'Copyright Assistance', *Bit.Listserv.Gutnberg*, 12 February 1992.

[125] Michael S. Hart, 'New Gutenberg Directors', *Bit.Listserv.Gutnberg*, 19 February 1992.

[126] Hart, 'Project Gutenberg Feb Newsletter'.

[127] Michael S. Hart to Book People mailing list, 'Project Gutenberg Needs You!', 1 May 1997.

providing others with core roles within the Project, Hart scaled it in ways he was unable to do alone.

Greg Newby, a Professor of Library and Information Sciences at the University of Illinois, was undoubtedly the most consequential volunteer. Hart met Newby in 1992, and the two forged a strong friendship over the Project. Newby began by digitising texts for the Project but soon grew into a more important role. In 2000, Newby was instrumental in Project Gutenberg's professionalisation with the formation of the Project Gutenberg Literary Archive Foundation and the subsequent integration of Distributed Proofreaders, created by Charles Franks to crowdsource the process of correcting digitised material. While outside of the period of study in this book, Newby's initiatives post-2000 to professionalise PG are responsible for its current standing within the community. Without this formalised structure, Hart was largely allowed to mythologise his own importance while relying on a smaller number of volunteers.

While Hart required a large amount of volunteers and equipment to keep up his digitisation schedule and desire to reach 10,000 books by 2001, the operation was not purely a technical one. The social and legal elements are equally important in constructing a successful digitisation project, especially without large-scale corporate or institutional investment that would be attached to later megaprojects including Google Books and HathiTrust. The legal and social elements are immediately embedded within these larger projects, but Hart had to develop the networks and know-how through bottom-up experimentation. He was only successful in building these partnerships *after* the 1990s, demonstrating the flaws in his claim to be the first major digitisation project. With such a small online community, it is easy to suggest that you were one of the first to digitise a text but the Project would only grow in reputation once it built a community.

The social elements of digitisation contributed significantly to the early growth of the Project. Several participants were interested in offering new content rather than improving pre-existing publications or posting something others had already completed. For example, Charles Keller sent an email to Hart in 1992 noting, 'After spending too much time on this etext I discovered a commercial source of this etext. I am going to invest my time and effort on the more 'obscure' of the popular literature to avoid this duplication.'[128] Keller's observation here is illuminating as he was not disappointed that the book already existed in the digital public domain but rather that users could purchase a copy. Many open access advocates favour reproducing commercially available material if it brought a free copy into circulation, but Keller appears to be interested in obscurity for the sake of increasing the overall number of texts in circulation.

5.4 Intellectual Property

Beyond the necessity of recruiting volunteers to digitise texts, Hart had to recruit subject-specific experts to ensure the initiative would thrive. As a result of his adept networking, Hart was also in a good position for legal advice. This had been a priority for him since Project Gutenberg stepped up a gear in the mid-1980s: after investing heavily in the ill-fated 1980s Shakespeare edition, Hart and his team of volunteers adopted a strict approach to copyright to avoid this wasted effort. That is not to say that early publications did not include copyrighted material but only with direct permission from the copyright holder. Mary Jensen Brandt was asked to focus on copyright clearance. She used her experience from Project Gutenberg to publish on the topic including an article 'Cohabiting with Copyright on the Nets' and the 1997 book *Does Your Project Have a Copyright Problem?: A Decision-making Guide for Librarians*. Brandt developed a rigorous workflow for ensuring a specific copy of a book was in the public domain even if the original publication met the criteria. This would occasionally include a more thorough check on the paragraph level to confirm that a text had not been changed from the original version but mostly required volunteers to send the copyright page to Brandt who verified that the text was in the public domain.

Hart was not above inflating the Project's strengths in copyright. For example, in April 1997, he braggadociously claimed that 'Project Gutenberg has possibly done more copyright research than any other Etext project'.[129]

---

[128] Charles Keller to Michael S. Hart, 'JUNGLE.TXT', 12 November 1992.

[129] Michael S. Hart to Book People mailing list, '!!!!!!Re: New Copyright Dates on Old Works and Scanning.', 1 April 1997.

While there is clear evidence that the group of volunteers in place by the late 1990s had a strong workflow for copyright clearance after early failures to publish an edition of Shakespeare's works, none of this had influenced legislation and in fact, the Project struggled to adapt to several major changes to copyright law over the 1990s regardless.

Hart's confidence often failed him in terms of international copyright law. In 1994, he was looking to expand the international appeal of the Project by suggesting that they were able to provide copyright advice beyond the United States. Nicolas Graner, a French volunteer, accepted this offer but after Mary Brandt Jensen responded that she did not have the relevant specialist knowledge, Graner wrote a despondent email asking what information was required.[130] As a result, Graner did not contribute a published text and Project Gutenberg did not have any French language content until the publication of Stendhal's *L'Abbesse De Castro* (#797) in January 1997. This was not the start of a large body of French work, at least in the original language, as only an additional 159 French language titles were released before the publication of *Magna Carta* as text 10,000 in March 2006. Nonetheless, within the Anglophone context, Jensen's work was formidable, ensuring that even though volunteers may send something to the Incoming server in vain, no problematic texts would be posted unless thoroughly scrutinised.

The early ideology of Project Gutenberg was driven by the type of texts it published that shifted between focusing on the public domain worldwide or just within the United States. In the early 1990s this workflow was in flux as evidenced by disclaimers posted with early versions of J.M. Barrie's *Peter Pan* and Herman Melville's *Moby Dick*. Melville's text simply missed the seventy-second chapter in early postings because no one could confirm if the chapter had been taken from a public domain version. *Peter Pan* initially contained a lengthy disclaimer suggesting that it was public domain in the United States, but its status was unclear elsewhere, 'particularly in members or former members of the British Commonwealth'.[131] As a result, Project Gutenberg both suggested that no one outside of the United States

---

[130] Graner to Hart, 'French Copyright', 20 September 1994.

[131] Barrie, *Peter Pan*.

downloaded the file and asserted copyright over the edition 'due to our preparations of several sources, our own research, and the inclusion of additions and explanations to the original sources'.[132] These challenges remain in 2022, although the written disclaimers have vanished, as A.A. Milne's *Winnie the Pooh* was published to celebrate its entry into the US public domain, while it remains protected by UK law until 2026, seventy years after Milne's death.

5.4.1 Reacting to New Copyright Legislation

Two changes to copyright law defined Project Gutenberg's approach to digitisation over the course of the 1990s. First, the Uruguay Round Agreements Act (URAA) of 1994 led to the United States complying with the General Agreement of Tariffs and Trades (GATT), a law that increased protection for third-party countries by allowing works that had slipped out of copyright in the United States to be re-registered.[133] As Robert Spoo argues, 'the American public domain has made a slow journey from exceptionalism to internationalism since the first U.S. copyright act of 1790', of which the GATT marked the final step.[134] The US public domain shrank in line with other countries rather than taking works out of the public domain through extending copyright terms. This complicated the Project's ability to post works published from outside of the United States as the copyright could be re-registered at any time. As a result, Hart applied stricter criteria to copyright clearance.

This caution turned out to be a wise idea as the late 1990s saw further dramatic changes to copyright law. The Sonny Bono Copyright Term Extension Act of 1998 had a seismic effect on copying on the Internet as well as for other creative industries. While it did not take work out of the public domain like GATT, the ACT froze the year works entered the public domain in the United States for twenty-one years, ensuring that publications from 1923 would not enter the public domain until 2019. While the

---

[132] Barrie, *Peter Pan*.

[133] Kennedy, 'GATT-out of the Public Domain'; U.S. Copyright Office, 'Notices of Restored Copyrights'.

[134] Spoo, *Without Copyrights*, 264.

primary effect of this change was the unavailability of new material to publish, there was also a secondary challenge for the Project's workflow: any copy of a text in the public domain published after 1922 would cause legal headaches if there were sufficient editorial changes to ensure it was no longer in the public domain.

James Joyce provides a useful case study for the effect of these changes. In April 1994, Jason Eisner offered Michael Hart a complete collection of Joyce's works that had just entered the public domain.[135] This included *Finnegans Wake*, a text that remains in copyright in the United States until 2035. Stephen James Joyce, the author's grandson and Estate's executor, had increasingly used copyright to defend what he perceived to be slights against his family's honour from the mid-1980s, largely arguing that discussing personal matters were against Joyce's *le droit moral* (moral rights).[136] While this focused primarily on unpublished manuscripts, it also affected the online availability of Joyce's works. His works originally entered the public domain in 1991 but by 1995, a change in law in the EU (Council Directive 93/98/EEC of 29 October 1993) ensured they reverted to private ownership. The current version of Joyce's *Ulysses* on Project Gutenberg was released in July 2003 demonstrating PG's strong beliefs that the material was in the public domain despite the long-term struggle within the Joycean community around that time.[137] This discrepancy could be part of a move towards a US-first approach to copyright clearance where worldwide rights were less important.

At the start of January 1996, 'by legislative fiat, the URAA gave to the first Paris edition of *Ulysses*, which had lain in the American public domain since April 1922, what had always eluded Joyce during his lifetime: complete copyright protection in the United States'.[138] While this only gave a temporary reprieve until 1998, the Sonny Bono Copyright Act ensured Joyce would remain out of reach until the 2020s as the current copyright

---

[135] Jason Eisner to Michael S. Hart, '!!!!!! Complete Works of Joyce: Further Info', 22 April 1993; Jason Eisner to Michael S. Hart, '!!!!!! James Joyce Etexts on Their Way', 20 May 1993.

[136] Shloss, 'Joyce's Will'. [137] Joyce, *Ulysses*.

[138] Spoo, *Without Copyrights*, 265.

protection was essentially frozen, ensuring no works would enter the public domain for 21 years between 1 January 1998 and 2019.[139] The Joyce Estate capitalised on this change, having previously failed to supplant an earlier version of the text with Hans Walter Gabler's genetic edition of the text in the 1980s.[140] After receiving $160,000 in funding from the Mellon Foundation for creating a prototype hypertext edition of just the 'Proteus' chapter of *Ulysses*, Michael Groden's project was suspended in 2003 'after the Joyce estate asked for $2 million just to begin discussions on use of the text'.[141]

These challenges, which were accelerated by savvy literary estates' increased knowledge of the potential threat of digital publishing, ensured that any digitisation project would need to develop robust workflows to ensure the material they were posting was not protected by copyright. As a first step, Project Gutenberg uploaders needed to complete a 'Form for Source Information Files' that recorded who produced the file, what edition it was based upon, and to send the Title Page and Verso (TP&V) to Mary Brandt Jensen, who would then verify the information prior to approval.[142] As the operation continued to grow, Hart started to collate this information into a Public Domain Register, in order to oversee this work.[143] While this was partially an avenue for ensuring volunteers knew their material had been cleared, the Public Domain Register doubled up as a tool for publicising what other volunteers were working on to avoid unnecessary duplication.

5.4.2 Protecting the Project's Intellectual Property

The Project engaged with intellectual property law beyond copyright. Unsurprisingly, Hart was protective of the Project Gutenberg brand,

---

[139] Spoo, *Without Copyrights*, 265–66.

[140] See Arnold, *The Scandal of Ulysses*, chap. 8. [141] 'Joyce as Hypertext'.

[142] Mark Fuller to Michael S. Hart, '1884–1890 Darby Bible (on Your Server Now)', 21 August 1992.

[143] Michael Hart to GUTNBERG. 'Copyrights, 1994' 31 December 1994, Michael S. Hart Papers at the University Archives, at the University of Illinois at Urbana-Champaign.

going as far as to trademark it in 2000.[144] The lengthy legal disclaimers at the top of many PG texts reflect this caution: 'no one owns a United States copyright on or for this work, so the Project (and you!) can copy and distribute it in the United States without permission and without paying copyright royalties. Special rules, set forth below, apply if you wish to copy and distribute this etext under the Project's 'PROJECT GUTENBERG' trademark'.[145] The trademark motioned towards Hart's understanding of the prestige of his project and wanting to protect this reputation. This was built upon a series of successful partnerships during the 1990s, looking at ways that commercial uses of PG would be financially rewarding for the longer-term sustainability of the Project.

This juxtaposition between posting public domain content yet requesting acknowledgement that the material came from Project Gutenberg can be seen as a precursor of Creative Commons and other forms of open licenses that include attribution as part of any re-use.[146] Despite the voluntary nature of the boilerplate, users were keen to signify the text came from Project Gutenberg in most instances. This insistence for provenance runs counter to the level of bibliographic attention paid to the initial digitisation process. The metadata about who digitised the text is often patchy and only certain digitisers are interested in also including information about the edition they used or the editorial process they undertook. This emphasises readability over fidelity, but, nonetheless, there are tensions when considering the various layers and their interactions with one another.

5.5 *Working with Other Projects*

Project Gutenberg was not the only community digitisation project and Hart was keen to ensure that he made the most of his networks to maintain his schedule. Occasionally these partners would be acknowledged in the preface to the Project Gutenberg editions. There is a shift throughout the 1990s from smaller amateur projects and work conducted within an academic context to initiatives that were clearly inspired by Hart's earlier work.

---

[144] Hart, 'Service Mark Principal Register'. [145] Carroll, *Alice's Adventures*.
[146] 'About CC Licenses'.

There are also several collaborations with for-profit corporations including Millennium Fulcrum and Enigma Corporation. This evidence corroborates Hart's loose commitment to principles of the public domain when it otherwise ensured he had enough content.

Table 1 shows the range of institutions, voluntary groups, and corporations working on public domain digitisation over the course of the 1990s and the increasing professionalisation as corporations began to see the value of selling these publications in digital form. Hart was keen to develop these networks to diversify the number of sources he relied on to meet his ambitious targets. He also engaged in taking content from other sources without acknowledgement, publicly noting that once the OTA started to distribute texts via FTP, he would be downloading them, removing the SGML and reuploading to Project Gutenberg.[147] Emails in his personal archive demonstrate that he followed through with this on some occasions too including a collection of Henry James novels and a copy of *Dracula*, both

Table 1 Acknowledged collaborators 1991–1999

Year	Credits
1991	On-Line Book Initiative
1992	The PaperLess Readers Club, Houston
1993	Internet Wiretap
1994	Center for Computer Analysis of Texts (CCAT) at the University of Pennsylvania, the Digital Daguerreian Archive Project
1995	Millennium Fulcrum
1996	Project Wittenberg
1997	World Library Inc
1998	Project Runeberg
1999	Enigma Corporation

---

[147] Michael S. Hart, 'Oxford Via FTP', *Bit.Listserv.Gutnberg*, 8 October 1992.

of which were provided by Judy Boss.[148] Some months, Hart would not have met his production targets without this formal and illicit re-use of others' material.

At other times, Hart claimed collaborators worked directly for PG rather than the original source. In his interview with Hamilton for *WIRED* Hart bragged about 'A group of 50 Russian academics [who] recently did Webster's Unabridged Dictionary by hand. The 45 million keystrokes took them six months, for which they were paid $5,000 by one of Hart's financial supporters'.[149] These claims do not hold up to closer scrutiny. The *Webster's Dictionary* digitisation was funded by MICRA Inc, a self-described 'small corporation in New Jersey primarily concerned with building lexical databases for use in Natural Language Understanding' in collaboration with the American and French Research on the Treasury of the French Language (ARTFL) Project out of the University of Chicago.[150] The dictionary may have been typed in manually by a team of Russians – the only corroborating evidence comes from the mention that 'much of this material was typed in by hand by non-native speakers of English'.[151] MICRA and ARTFL digitised the dictionary as part of a larger collaboration on semantic markup for reference texts, and Hart was only working as a distributor. Cassidy hoped that sharing the text via the Project would demonstrate the potential for low-cost and free text databases.[152] In fact, several parts of the original text (revised in the following year) contained omissions that were under copyright.[153]

5.6 Conclusion

Licensing content from other publishers demonstrates the nature of the Project's early development. Hart was a deft networker, able to draw in partners and support from a range of relevant collaborators, but not much of

[148] Judy Boss to Michael S. Hart, 'Frost poems, OTA, all caps', 19 August 1993; Judy Boss to Michael S. Hart, 'Re: Dracula', 26 October 1993.

[149] Hamilton, 'Hart of the Gutenberg Galaxy'.

[150] Cassidy, 'MICRA'; Olson, 'Webster Search Form'.

[151] Webster, *The Gutenberg Webster's*.

[152] Patrick Cassidy to Michael S. Hart, 'Webster 1913 – format'. 20 January 1995.

[153] Webster, *The Gutenberg Webster's*.

this work was conducted for the sole benefit of the Project. This required a high degree of awareness of the field which should not be ignored, but it does not translate to Hart's model of patronage that he played up whenever he was trying to claim to be the spearhead of a movement. Many of MICRA and ARTFL's aims stood in direct opposition to Hart's ideology as they wanted to introduce as much markup as possible, as noted in correspondence between Cassidy and Hart.[154] The spin apparent in Hart's acquisition of *Webster* reflects a wider pattern within the early development of Project Gutenberg: Hart did not recruit enough volunteers to maintain his ambitious schedule so he asked other groups to share their content. A *WIRED* article from 1997 placed the number of volunteers at 1,000 but only helped sporadically.[155] As a consequence, a core group of dedicated volunteers helped to shape the course of the Project, which reflected their own interests rather than a more representative section of the public domain.

---

[154] Patrick Cassidy to Michael S. Hart, 'Webster 1913 – format'. 20 January 1995.
[155] Silberman, 'A Thousand Classics'.

6 Digital Publishing Collective

The importance of labour donated to Project Gutenberg is impossible to overstate. Nonetheless, Hart pushed a narrative that he was responsible for the Project's success and its failures would reflect poorly on him: 'I can't really help proofreading every book that Project Gutenberg does, because my reputation and that of Project Gutenberg is on the line'.[156] At the time, he had only distributed twenty-six texts in thirty-one years where once he allowed others to proofread titles, over 60,000 were published in less than thirty years. The rhetoric belies Hart's mission at the time. He was actively recruited volunteers, having 'travelled to the American Library Association's midwinter meeting to proselytize for e-books and Project Gutenberg'. At the conference, he vowed, "There will be 10,000 Machine-Readable-Texts available by Dec. 31, 2000, even if I [have] to make them all myself"'.[157] Hart attempted to leverage his perceived charisma to encourage others to volunteer but too often this veered into the territory where his comments centred his efforts over a vastly complex machine. Hart required many volunteers to meet his ambitious schedule. In a post to bit.listserv. gutnberg called '1993 schedule', he outlined his plans to double production each year to meet his goal of 10,000 digitised titles by its 30th anniversary so he could retire, a goal he never achieved.[158] Despite the in-flux of volunteers, he fell short of this target, posting book 4,300 – James Joyce's *Ulysses* – in December 2001. For many of the early years where the pace was one book per week, production exceeded these expectations leading to celebratory notes at the beginning of the title. The Production team often used landmark publications to boost the number posted in a month. For example, text 1000, Dante's *Divine Comedy* was published in four different forms with each major section appearing separately, accounting for all twelve of the texts released that month.[159]

Nonetheless, the early Web in combination with mailing lists and Usenet ensured that Project Gutenberg thrived in the mid-1990s. As a result, Hart

---

[156] Hart, 'PS'.   [157] Peters, *Idealist*, 107.

[158] Hart, 'Not a Newsletter'. *Bit.Listserv.Gutnberg*. 7 January 1992.

[159] Dante, *Divina Commedia*.

looked to reset PG's direction. In a posting to Bit.Listserv.Gutnberg in October 1993, he outlined his goals as focusing on:

1. Light Literature
2. Heavy Literature
3. Reference Books
4. Computer Books
5. Scientific Data[160]

Aside from the bizarre classification of 'light' and 'heavy' literature, there is a clear split in focus between the republication of canonical public domain work that became the Project's *modus operandi* during the 1990s and Hart's broader interests in the early development of the Project as a repository for various types of information online. The latter three categories veered into copyrighted material and were more prevalent in the early 1990s. In just the first one hundred files, all published before the end of 1993, titles included Brendan P. Kehoe's *Zen and the Art of the Internet*, James Daly's edited collection of *Workshop on Electronic Texts: Proceedings, 9-10 June 1992*, the text of the NAFTA Agreement and 'Price/Cost Indexes from 1989; Estimated to 2010', as well as lengthy numerical documents on 'The First 100,000 Prime Numbers' and 'The Square Root of 2'. Overall, 12 per cent of publications posted by 1993 were from the final three categories, a proportion that was maintained for the following 200 titles but petered out by around 1995 with a brief resurgence in 1996 where Jerry Bonnell and Robert Nemiroff posted a series of square roots. By the turn of 1998, the Project's focus had almost entirely turned from requesting permission to post in-copyright work to concentrating on the public domain titles that it has since become synonymous with.

Hart reflected on the importance of collaboration when posting his 1993 schedule:

> Let's face it, the day when a single person could do a majority of a year's work of Project Gutenberg is long gone, and what has been the height of disorganization since

---

[160] Michael S. Hart, '1993 Schedule', *Bit.Listserv.Gutnberg*, 1 October 1993.

> 1971 is going to have to be a little more organized each year,
> if we are going to double production every year as we have
> been.[161]

While he did not meet his most ambitious goals, the Project accelerated its growth until it stabilised towards the end of the 1990s, largely due to Hart's renewed focus on collaboration.

6.1 Early Attempts to Diversify Publications

The Project's early experiments with works beyond 'the classics' expanded beyond text, spurred on by the Web's ability to transmit non-text-based formats. These included audio and video files such as Ludwig van Beethoven's Symphony No. 5 in C minor, Opus 67 (#156) and NASA's *Motion Pictures of the Apollo 11 Lunar Landing* (#116). Both files were published in small scale version, appropriate for the dial up connections of 1994. Beethoven's Symphony appeared as a MIDI file while the *Lunar Landing* is available as both a low-resolution AVI and an MPG file. MIDI, or Musical Instrument Digital Interface, is the more interesting of the formats as it represents a low-bandwidth method of providing complex instructions via alphanumeric means. Rather than presenting a specific recording of the Symphony, MIDI instead provides instructions for instruments in a software package to interpret. In this way, it can be seen as the equivalent of HTML where the structure of information is more important than its final representation. This reduced the file size dramatically, which was the goal of the early development of MIDI as an interoperable protocol for transmitting signals between digital musical devices. The Project would continue to sporadically publish music files, although as bandwidth continue, to increase, these started to take the form of MP3s rather than MIDIs, leaving these files as interesting historical anomalies.

Branching out into these other types of media and genres reveals Hart's broader repositioning of the Project in the early years of the Web. Through accepting a range of material, PG could become a repository or archive for the sort of work conducted elsewhere. This can be seen in both the

---

[161] Hart, '1993 Schedule.'

collaborative arrangements I discussed in the previous chapter and Hart's desire to include texts other than strict digitisations. For example, Hart included several versions of the CIA World Factbook in the mid-1990s to ensure this material was available to a wider audience. Hart was subscribed to the Government Publishing Office mailing list at the time which sent notifications of new public domain government publications. He then reposted this material on PG to increase the audience of both the site, through the potential for discoverability, and the publication.

Due to the lack of institutional support, Project Gutenberg has haphazard coverage based upon materials accessed and scanned by volunteers rather than the more omnivorous behaviour of Google Books and the Internet Archive. This approach introduced the biases of the digitisers into the curation process with prominent volunteers frequently focusing on specific, often canonised, authors from the nineteenth century with large back catalogues that were easily accessible. Similar biases can be observed in mass digitisation projects such as Google Books, but these are less traceable back to individuals due to their scale.[162] While there was some curation that ran against this around core events, the Project took a long time to represent a more diverse range of authors.

Between 1992 and 1996, Martin Luther King Jr Day was marked with the release of a significant publication related to black history, starting with *The Narrative of Life of Frederick Douglass* (#24) in 1992. The following two years also featured a Frederick Douglass publication, with the 1994 publication of *Collected Articles of Frederick Douglass* (#99) featuring an explicit request for more material published to celebrate historically significant dates.[163] Judy Boss, a Professor of Native American Studies, led the efforts to expand the diversity of publications in 1995 and 1996 with the release of *The Martin Luther King Jr Day 1995 Memorial Issue* (#207) and W. E. B. Du Bois's *The Soul of Black Folk* in 1996. The effort dissipated after 1996, although in 2019, David Widger produced 'Index of Project Gutenberg Works on Black History' (#58,975) to celebrate Black History Month. Only 58 titles are indexed, indicating stagnation in volunteers digitising

---

[162] Pechenick, Danforth, and Dodds, 'Characterizing the Google Books Corpus'.

[163] Douglass, 'Collected Articles'.

relevant material even during the first wave of Black Lives Matter protests. The earliest attempts at formalising celebrating important dates largely failed due to the difficulty of scheduling publications when the overall output was so low and Hart would often be keen to publish early if something was ready. Furthermore, the emphasis on landmark dates in these early years also ensured that Black authors were primarily published in the first two months of the year rather than integrated throughout the schedule. There is a degree of tokenism to releasing content published by women or BIPOC on special occasions rather than embedding this into a broader publication strategy. This reflects Hart's free market approach to digitisation that ensured content at the cost of a more equitable form of curation. Once the easiest to find and digitise texts had been uploaded, Project Gutenberg began to look further for source material.

Project Gutenberg's digitisation workflow reduced the barriers to locating source material, although this led to uneven results. Unlike several major early corporate digitisation efforts such as Early English Books Online (EEBO) or Eighteenth-Century Collection Online (ECCO), Project Gutenberg went direct to the source for the digitisation rather than working with an intermediary such as microfilm.[164] The resulting digitisations were only limited by the equipment and technique, rather than bound by the quality of the transitionary medium. It also highlighted the challenges of accessing relevant source material. Without the institutional or corporate resources, Hart and his volunteers' curation methods were ad hoc, relying on whatever public domain material they could find. In a post to the Book People mailing list entitled 'Project Gutenberg Needs You!' in May 1997, Hart stated: 'We need people to hunt through libraries or bookstores for editions that we can use to legally prepare our Electronic Texts.'[165] Hart relied on serendipity and availability as core principles for the rollout of digitisations. It did not matter what texts were available if volunteers hit targets and he could legally post them online.

Hart's philosophy of digitisation, focusing on extracting the text as ASCII, reduced the fetishism of the original prioritised by similar

---

[164] Mak, 'Archaeology'; Gregg, *Old Books*.

[165] Hart to Book People mailing list, 'Project Gutenberg Needs You!', 1 May 1997.

digitisation projects. While EEBO and ECCO depended on access to high-quality originals, even if reprints from near the original point of publication, Project Gutenberg had no preference. Even facsimiles were not necessarily essential. If the text was deemed to be in the public domain, Project Gutenberg was happy to host it. This was partially a pragmatic decision. Given most originals or early print runs would only be available in major research libraries and often within the confines of rare books and special collections, Gutenberg volunteers were unlikely to be able to access a large quantity of pre-twentieth-century material. Nonetheless, it had an overall chilling effect on matters of provenance and textual scholarship. Hart clearly understood material bibliography through interactions with his father, but between his insistence on plain text, discussed in Chapter 3, and encouraging others to digitise materials, he became less interested in acknowledging provenance. This process accelerated as distributed workflows required users to work with different editions of the same text.

6.2 Pursuing Individual Interests

Ensuring volunteers were interested in contributing was just as important as having an engaged audience. To maintain the cohesion of the Project Gutenberg digital publishing collective, Hart and, at a later date, Greg Newby had to ensure a balance between regular contributions and offering volunteers the freedom to pursue their own interests and therefore produce material. By 2004, Hart and Newby had established the Principle of Minimal Regulation/Administration. In this document, they concluded, 'The only barrier that Project Gutenberg seeks to maintain is the one that keeps notions such as dogmatism, perfectionism, elitism, format restrictions, content restrictions and so forth from restricting the freedom of people to create, read and distribute the eBooks they are interested in.'[166] Such a statement clearly follows the idealism embedded in Weber's choice of the term 'collective', but there are many contradictory factors that demonstrate this was not always the case. For example, as we have seen above, Hart had strong opinions about formats that shaped the materials available via PG. As with many statements claiming neutrality, the purported

---

[166] Hart and Newby, 'Principle of Minimal Regulation'.

'freedom' only extends in certain directions, leading to a corpus skewed towards those with the ability to locate, digitise, and correct material.

6.3 Gaps in Coverage

Hart's focus on growth had unfortunate, yet expected, consequences: The sorts of works available demonstrate the uneven distribution of resources. Project Gutenberg clearly benefitted from its early lack of curatorial direction, encouraging volunteers to follow their interests rather than requesting specific texts were digitised. This did, however, lead to some clear blind spots as the content posted often reflected the demographic of the volunteers more than the full diversity of the public domain. As Nanna Bonde Thylstrup argues, 'there is precious little diversity in the official map of mass digitization, even in those projects that emerge bottom-up'.[167] Unfortunately, before 2000 there was a clear disparity in the number of works authored by white men compared to any other demographic. Given the Project's scope and resources, this is perhaps not unsurprising as the lack of diversity reflects the canon of major Anglophone languages. Since 'canonical' works are more likely to be reprinted, there is a greater likelihood that volunteers will be able to access these titles. Coupled with volunteers following their interests, this initially led to a homogenous set of authors up until Distributed Proofreaders and the necessity to publish niche content offered some course correction.

Authors from Great Britain and the United States are over-represented in the early corpus, and to a lesser extent continue to be, due to the regional interests of those working on the digitisations. It is often easier to find early publications of materials in one's own language and national context. Individuals had a clear preference for their favourite authors rather than ensuring the content reflected a more inclusive kind of digitisation. For example, David Price, the most prominent digitiser in my dataset, contributed 304 texts between May 1995 and December 1999. Of these publications, 268 (88 per cent) were written by men, mostly prolific authors such as Robert Louis Stevenson and Charles Dickens.

---

[167] Thylstrup, *Politics of Mass Digitization*, 7–8.

The gender breakdown of all titles published before 2000 (n=2,377) demonstrates some of the coverage gaps in the early digitisation efforts. Men authored 83 per cent of publications, while only 13 per cent of publications had at least one female co-author. The remaining eighty-eight publications did not have an explicitly labelled male or female author. Several of the unidentified authors are likely to be male as these documents are largely works such as the US Constitution and *The Book of Mormon*, but I only count the authors listed in the metadata. Figure 2 outlines the change in the proportion of publications per gender over time. The number of titles with male authors falls substantially in the second one hundred publications because the Project Gutenberg edition of the *Encyclopaedia Britannica* takes up twenty publication numbers but only has one dedicated entry, leading to a gap in the overall data. The second hundred books show a correction for the number of women published by the Project with the first publication of authors such as Jane Austen, but this percentage diminishes slightly over time. There are fewer unidentified authors as the Project matured which again was replaced by more publications by male authors. Hart willingly prioritised volume over equity in his early acquisition strategy, which led to an insurmountable gender gap.

Despite this gender imbalance, there were initiatives to increase the visibility of women's writers online, albeit often only tangentially to Project

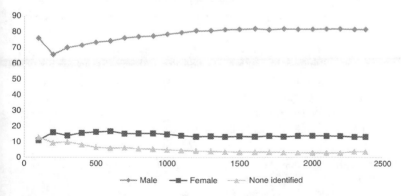

Figure 2 Percentage of titles published by gender

Gutenberg. Most prominently, scholars at Brown University launched the Women Writers Project back in 1988.[168] There were clear efforts to increase the number of women authors represented on the website, but these were small-scale projects without the resources of major digitisers who made up the bulk of early submissions. For example, in October 1997, Martha Summerhayes's *Vanished Arizona*, included the comment that 'this etext was prepared by a team of Arizona women'.[169] These represented outliers from other amateur digitisation projects that had developed in response to a specific issue rather than more omnivorous approach of PG.

There are instances where Hart intentionally produced material for a wider audience. For example, Frances Hodgson Burnett's *The Secret Garden* was published in March 1994 'In honor of Lisa Hart's 9th birthday'.[170] There was some knowledge of the gender biases baked within the Project's core design and philosophy, but this was never engaged with through policies and auditing, leading to a great imbalance between representations of gender and race within the corpus that has had a substantial impact on re-uses of Project Gutenberg I discuss in the next chapter.

Pennsylvania University hosted Mary Mark Ockerbloom's 'Celebration of Women's Writers' from 1994 which had a more direct impact on Project Gutenberg.[171] Some of the titles published by Gutenberg in 1997 and 1998 contain bibliographic data suggesting that 'This book has been put on-line as part of the BUILD-A-BOOK Initiative at the Celebration of Women Writers'.[172] As with many of the other early successes for the Project, this work was conducted on the edges and was only republished rather than instigated by Hart. He was a strong networker and was able to use his connections to republish work undertaken elsewhere. Often these other projects would have a clearer social justice perspective and would therefore address the blindspots within Hart's work.

[168] Northeastern University Women Writers Project, 'WWP History'.
[169] Summerhayes, *Vanished Arizona*. [170] Burnett, *The Secret Garden*.
[171] Ockerbloom, 'Celebration of Women Writers'.
[172] Addams, *20 Years at Hull House*.

6.4 Conclusion

Project Gutenberg's digitisation strategies depended on both sociolegal and technological factors to scale up from posting one text a year throughout the 1970s to over 750 per annum in 2000. A combination of an eager volunteer base matched with legal know-how, acquired after some early failures, ensured the Project had a consistent drip of new material to post. Unfortunately, the lack of curatorial oversight and reliance on volunteers to source their own materials led to uneven coverage of different authors, reflecting the demographic of the digitisers rather than the full range of possible works to digitise. Some of these problems have been corrected in more recent work, but overall PG remains focused on 'canonical' works of Western literature. In recent years, the growth of the public domain has given rise to new opportunities to broaden the scope of acquisitions that may bear fruit in future years.

7 Anti-Platform: Project Gutenberg's Lasting Influence

In 2019, Project Gutenberg hit the milestone of 60,000 books, relatively insignificant compared to the Internet Archive's 21 million books, but a large amount for a community project. Despite being eclipsed in size by other mass digitisation initiatives, Project Gutenberg remains one of the most recognisable names, especially over other long-running rivals such as the Oxford Text Archive. In this concluding chapter, I consider how hagiographical efforts have shaped our historical understanding of Project Gutenberg's significance. Following the recontextualisation of Hart's work and the Project more specifically, the chapter offers a new appraisal of the significance of Project Gutenberg. To this end, I suggest that rather than a platform, Project Gutenberg acts as an 'anti-platform' where content has spread far beyond the boundaries and logic of Hart's original intentions that the concept of a traditional publisher or platform is difficult reconcile with Project Gutenberg's current position within the digitisation community.

As I have discussed in the preceding chapters, Hart was a strong networker. He was able to seek out volunteers with specialisms in his areas of weakness. This level of networking was required for creating a project from the ground up, but it also had the consequence that it was not a stable entity. Even from the early days of Project Gutenberg, Hart relied on reposting content from elsewhere to boost the number of titles available. This led to the creation of a more spreadable type of digitisation project despite texts containing extensive legal boilerplate asking others to include attribution to Project Gutenberg.

7.1 Interoperability and Spreadability

Hart's approach to content prioritised interoperability. As Bonde Thylstrup notes: 'More than denoting a technical fact, then, interoperability emerges today as an infrastructural logic, one that promotes openness, modularity, and connectivity.'[173] Project Gutenberg's overall setup was always designed with these principles implicitly in mind. For example, the fact that PG did not have a stable online presence and even when it found an institutional home

---

[173] Thylstrup, *Politics of Mass Digitization*, 68.

encouraged others to recreate their own infrastructure to ensure the content was available in as many regions as possible. This can be seen through how Project Gutenberg spreads across different platforms including mirrors or sister projects, integration into other platforms, and use as a training set for machine learning.

Project Gutenberg's increased spreadability also depended on the loose definition of its boundaries. The current website, Gutenberg.org, was only registered in 1996. Before then, the Project moved between different servers on the Web, FTP, and Gopher. Others were, and still are, encouraged to mirror PG content ensuring that there was never one definitive source. In fact, the Project's own approach to file management also demonstrates a lack of consistency with some older files retained but not all of them. This approach to definitive copies and authorised archives combines to a liberal approach to spreadability. There is a greater emphasis on ensuring texts are available online than that every download comes directly from the Gutenberg servers, as long as the material does not use the trademark without gaining permission beforehand.

This mirroring can also be seen in the national efforts that emerged in line with Project Gutenberg over the course of the 1990s. For example, the August 1999 release of *Bibeln, Gamla och Nya Testamentet* was coordinated with Project Runeberg with the tagline 'Nordic literature, art on the Internet since 1992', which is still running as of 2022.[174] Others took inspiration from PG to focus on a niche interest rather than a nation's corpus. Most prominently, Philipp Melanchthon's *Die Augsburger Confession* was part of Project Witternberg, led by Rev Robert E. Smith from Concordia Theological Seminary, 'dedicated to posting on the internet a cross-section of classic and historic texts written by Lutherans'.[175] While not every digitised text was shared with PG, these projects were at least spiritually indebted to Hart's approach to digitisation and the records of early Gutenberg digitisations effectively maintain those links.

7.2 Input and Output

Project Gutenberg's commitment to interoperability, made possible by the permissive licensing permissions discussed in Section 5.4.2, led to its

---

[174] Project Gutenberg, ed., *Bibeln*; 'Project Runeberg'.

[175] Melanchthon, *Die Augsburger Confession*; Smith, 'What Is Project Wittenberg?'

integration into a number of publishing and academic research workflows. We can categorise these reuses as either *input*, work aimed at improving the materials available on Project Gutenberg and affiliate sites, or *output*, where third parties use PG's publications to create something new. There is an asymmetric balance between inputs and outputs: successful inputs require the consent of Project Gutenberg whereas anyone can reuse its content. Nonetheless, some of the most transformational partnerships have emerged from new inputs that improve the quality of PG's publications.

7.2.1 Input

Distributed Proofreaders, an exemplar of this focus on interoperability, became a central strand for developing relationships between different partners and ensuring greater transparency in the process of digitisation. Charles Frank founded the platform in 2000 with the sole purpose of aiding workflows for PG. While it briefly became an official PG site in 2002, by May 2006 it had 'become a separate legal entity and continues to maintain a strong relationship with PG'.[176] In May 2021, the footer of the website boasted of '485 active users in the past twenty-four hours [. . .] 2,760 active users in the past 30 days' as well as over 42,000 completed titles, 2,100 in progress and 600 in the early stages of proofreading.[177] Each title goes through multiple stages of scrutiny before being sent to Project Gutenberg. In total, there are three rounds of initial crowdsourced proofreading before formatting is applied and then corrected. Finally, volunteers conduct a collective 'smooth reading' looking for any final errors before it is passed on to a single 'Post-Processor' who reads through the text attentively one more time to ensure all errors have been removed.[178]

Leonard Richardson and the New York Public Library Lab considered how to improve the discoverability of the Project Gutenberg titles within their e-book borrowing collection.[179] Richardson notes that while the metadata accompanying PG e-books is generally useful, it lacks two of the most important elements for library users: an attractive cover and

---

[176] 'Distributed Proofreaders'.   [177] 'Distributed Proofreaders'.

[178] 'DP Walkthrough'.

[179] Richardson, 'Project Gutenberg Books Are Real'; 'Generative EBook Covers'.

a summary of the contents.[180] The covers were automatically generated through a process borrowed from a classic piece of Commodore 64 code: '10 PRINT CHR$(205.5+RND(1)); : GOTO 10'.[181] Using this basic principle, the cover generator produces an abstract set of shapes to create something recognisably unique rather than the default Gutenberg book cover. The NYPL Lab shared the code so users could generate their own unique cover. The summary was more challenging and reflects a bottleneck in workflows. As Richardson notes, Distributed Proofreaders often created summaries, but those were not being pulled through to the final publications on Project Gutenberg.[182] This remains an unresolved issue as the DP and PG metadata are still separate.

7.2.2 Output

PG continued to find new partnerships and reuses in the last two decades to account for more recent trends in digital distribution and consumption. Two of the more interesting re-uses come from Wattpad and GITenberg. Wattpad started as a writing platform in 2006 but rapidly diversified into a range of business models, encapsulating what Claire Parnell terms a media ecosystem.[183] In order to boost the number of texts available, Wattpad formed a partnership with Gutenberg in January 2007 for users to access the texts via the Wattpad website.[184] This was a curious partnership since the authors present on Project Gutenberg are largely dead. The deal instead brought a social element to Project Gutenberg texts at the height of Web 2.0 mania. Users could now comment on these texts and interact with other Wattpad readers. This greatly benefitted Wattpad's early development as it boosted the number of available texts by tens of thousands, but the social elements for these publications have not been used by most readers on Wattpad.

GITenberg is another useful example of how others are extending PG's influence through reconceptualising how publications can be displayed.

---

[180] Richardson, 'Project Gutenberg Books Are Real'.

[181] See Montfort et al., *10 PRINT* for an overview of this code.

[182] Richardson, 'Project Gutenberg Books are Real'.

[183] Parnell, 'Mapping the Entertainment Ecosystem'; See also Ramdarshan Bold, 'The Return of the Social Author'.

[184] Wattpad, 'Gutenberg'.

Since Hart was adamant on ASCII formatting, this allowed others to reuse the raw data for different purposes. The Free Ebook Foundation, based out of New Jersey, launched GITenberg as a way of linking Gutenberg texts to Git workflows.[185] Git is a version management package that tracks changes and allows re-use in various ways. Converting Gutenberg files to Git ensures a greater degree of spreadability since re-uses can be linked, forked, and other mechanisms from within the Git syntax. While the package has not been used extensively, it offers a proof-of-concept for how PG content might be reused.

7.3 Extractivism

Despite the various publication-based re-uses of Project Gutenberg, its influence has been greater as a *corpus* (a bundle of texts) rather than a library of e-books. This links to Hart's original positioning of PG as a collection of e-texts, as part of his strong adherence to plain text and 'ASCII imperialism' discussed in Chapter 3, before the later pivot to calling them e-books. Given the size and ready availability of PG texts compared to other similar large datasets, it is unsurprising that it has become the foundations for many Machine Learning (ML) or Natural Language Processing (NLP) projects. The large volume of text provides ready-made examples of patterns within language connected to some useful metadata that highlights the rough date of publication along with other characteristics. For example, Richard Bean used the corpus to solve unsolved encrypted messages in historical documents.[186] Likewise, the popularity of PG as a corpus has led several projects to pre-process the data for various purposes.[187] The Project has also been used as a meta-corpus to test the reliability of other corpora such as in Jiang et al.'s research that compares PG with HathiTrust to assess the negative influence of non-corrected OCR in comparison to a highly corrected corpus.[188] As PG has been overshadowed as a consumer e-book site since the launch of the Kindle

---

[185] 'Free Ebook Foundation'; Woodworth, 'GITenberg'.

[186] Bean, 'Use of Project Gutenberg'.

[187] Gerlach and Font-Clos, 'A Standardized Project Gutenberg Corpus'; Csaky and Recski, 'The Gutenberg Dialogue Dataset'.

[188] Jiang et al., 'The Gutenberg-HathiTrust Parallel Corpus'.

and Kobo, it is likely that the scholarly approaches of PG and its embedded-ness within a range of experimental datasets will be the longer influence of the Project.

This level of re-use comes with its own set of problems, however, as it ensures an extractivist approach to the content that largely ignores the impor-tance of the original contributors. Arguably, this brought Project Gutenberg full circle as it ensured that it could be positioned as an e-text corpus rather than a collection of e-books. Of course, a researcher's choice to use PG is pragmatic when access to other similar large-scale digitised corpora, including Google Books and HathiTrust, comes with far greater restrictions. PG has just become the default because of its level of spreadability. Since many of these re-uses strip the files of their headers and footers, the datasets obfuscate their provenance. It is worth noting how, as with other machine learning datasets, the use of Project Gutenberg just amplifies the biases of the original corpus.

Text-based digital humanities research can often rely on extractivist research methods. Most prominently, the early wave of 'distant reading' led by the Stanford Literary Lab exemplifies how computational methods reflect Hart's rejection of everything but plain text.[189] In a lengthy rebuttal of these methods, Katherine Bode argues: 'Where distant reading and macroanalysis are celebrated – or decried – for their departure from close reading, these approaches share a disregard for textual scholarship and an assumption that literary works are stable and singular entities.'[190] Bode advocates instead for a model of understanding digital humanities through the lens of scholarly editions. Extractivism is equally prevalent in print-on-demand publishing. As Whitney Trettien documents with a case study of John Milton's *Areopagitica*, the existence of free-to-reuse digitised texts via Project Gutenberg and similar sites has led to a range of low-quality publications that simply extract the text from the Project, and other public domain digitisation sites, without any editorial oversight.[191] The poor quality of these publications reminds us that PG's texts require both editorial and production intervention, and therefore added value, before they are transformed into sellable trade commodities.

---

[189] 'Stanford Literary Lab'.   [190] Bode, 'Equivalence of "Close"', 91.
[191] Trettien, 'Deep History of Electronic Textuality'.

These new reuses and the removal of provenance, as well as Project Gutenberg's issues around version control, demonstrate the importance of historiographical approaches to such e-book repositories, especially around the processes of their creation and maintenance. These accounts help contexualise the labour and infrastructure involved in delivering and reading a digitised e-book. The most popular scholarship on e-books remains focused on the supposed comprehension gap between reading on-screen and in-print. We need to move beyond this binary: exploring processes in relation to products ensures we can look at the larger effects of digital publishing on the industry more broadly. Despite the difficulty of acquiring evidence from the early decades, focusing on historical developments enables a longer view of the field rather than assuming the Kindle appeared with no precedents.

7.4 The Future of Project Gutenberg?

Greg Newby and the Project Gutenberg Literary Archive Foundation have steered the direction of the Project since Hart's death in September 2011. It has continued to grow, albeit at a slower rate, due to the successes of the Distributed Proofreaders programme. In April 2021, Project Gutenberg posted its 65,000th publication: Agnes M. Clerke's *Familiar Studies in Homer*.[192] Nonetheless, the digital publishing ecosystem of 2021 is vastly different to the launch of Wattpad and the Kindle in the late 2000s, let alone 1971. In the age of Google Books, HathiTrust, and other mass digitisation initiatives, is there still a place for a mid-sized, community-driven project? The more permissive licensing of Project Gutenberg and its reuse within the machine learning and digital humanities communities suggest that there is an audience, as well as the download figures for the more popular works. There is also substantial evidence of community bonds in projects such as Distributed Proofreaders. While the scale has grown beyond the original coterie in the early 1990s, it is not so insurmountably large that it renders the community meaningless.

There are also incentives in terms of producing new content. Now that the freeze of the release of new public domain material legislated by the Copyright Extension Act in the United States has expired, there is a wealth of material that enters the public domain on 1st January of each year. While

[192] Clerke, *Familiar Studies*.

the most popular texts from the Modernist years are readily available, there is a goldmine of less popular material from the 1920s and 1930s that Gutenberg can seek to capitalise on over the next couple of decades. To test this hypothesis, I took a snapshot of the last twenty titles produced by Distributed Proofreaders on 31 May 2021 (table 2) to look at what kind of material is being published on Project Gutenberg in the early 2020s, based upon a randomly selected week, and assess if there has been a shift in curatorial perspective. All twenty titles were published on the week commencing 21 May 2021, demonstrating the increased production rate of Distributed Proofreading.

While only a small snapshot of the 2,870 books posted to PG in 2021, these twenty books nonetheless reveal some broader shifts in its acquisition patterns. Surprisingly, only two of the titles come from the newly public domain titles from 1923 and 1924. In fact, several of the titles were initially published in 1950s pulp science fiction magazines including *Imagination Stories of Science and Fantasy*. These titles may be part of the public domain due to a loophole in copyright legislation where work without an explicit copyright declaration published before 1989 with no indication of renewal would automatically enter the public domain. This is a risky strategy but demonstrates the confidence of volunteers to establish public domain material in spite of some of the more arcane elements of copyright law.

The pre-1925 titles show further shifts. Most importantly, most of these titles were sourced from external sites, including the Internet Archive and HathiTrust, as well as imaging from prominent national libraries such as the Library of Congress and the Bibliothèque nationale de France. This shows how the digitisation landscape has changed since the early 1990s. Now there are several industry and national efforts to scan in images of books that then other sites such as Project Gutenberg can use as the foundations for text extraction. Project Gutenberg's aim to store material already available elsewhere shifts away from Charles Keller's concerns around novelty to viewing it as a Lots of Copies Keeps Stuff Safe (LOCKSS)-style repository, which relies on multiple organisations holding the same material rather than relying on a single point of failure.[193] Using these primary sources means

---

[193] 'LOCKSS'.

Table 2 Twenty most recent Project Gutenberg publications via Distributed Proofreaders. 31 May 2021

Author	Title	Language	Publication Date	Subject [as defined by PG]	Notes on Source
John Randolph Neal	*Disunion and Restoration in Tennessee*	EN	1899	Reconstruction (U.S. history, 1865–1877) – Tennessee	PhD thesis. Images from Internet Archive (IA)
Mrs Margaret Oliphant	*The Primrose Path*	EN	1878	Fife (Scotland) – Fiction	Images from IA
Jean d'Arras	*Mélusine*	FR	1478	Melusine (Legendary character) – Romances	'This file was produced from images generously made available by The Internet Archive/ Canadian Libraries and the Bibliothèque nationale de France (BnF/Gallica) at http://gallica.bnf.fr'[194]

194 d'Arras, *Mélusine*.

Author	Title	Language	Year	Subject	Source
James Mars	*Life of James Mars, a Slave Born and Sold in Connecticut*	EN	1869	Slavery – Connecticut	HathiTrust Digital Library
Samuel Raymond Scottron	*Chinese vs. Negroes as American Citizens*	EN	1899	African Americans – Colonization – South America	Library of Congress
John Morison Copeland	*The Trail of the Swinging Lanterns*	EN	1918	Railroads – Canada	Internet Archive
N. Sokolov	*The Last Days of the Romanovs*	EN	1920	Nicholas II, Emperor of Russia, 1868–1918	Internet Archive/ American Libraries.
A.D. Mayo	*American Dangers and Duties*	EN	1861	Slavery – United States – History	Library of Congress
Randall Garrett	*Kill Me if You Can!*	EN	1957	Dictatorship – Fiction	[Transcriber's Note: This etext was produced from Imagination Stories of Science and Fantasy June 1957 Extensive research did not uncover any evidence that the U.S. copyright on this publication was renewed.][195]

[195] Tenneshaw, 'Kill Me If You Can!'.

Table 2 (cont.)

Author	Title	Language	Publication Date	Subject [as defined by PG]	Notes on Source
Mark Reinsberg	The Three Thieves of Japetus	EN	1957	Criminals – Fiction	As above.
J.-B.-J. Champagnac	Chronique du crime et de l'innocence, tome 6/8	FR	1833	Criminals – France	Imagination Stories of Science and Fantasy
Robert Silverberg	Woman's World	EN	1957	Sex role – Fiction	Serial publication
Robert Silverberg	Six Frightened Men	EN	1957	Outer space – Exploration – Fiction	Imagination Stories of Science and Fantasy
Alfred Döblin	Die beiden Freundinnen und ihr Giftmord	DE	1924	Women murderers – Germany – Berlin – History – 20th century	HathiTrust Digital Library
Robert W. Krepps	Beware, the Usurpers!	EN	1951	Human-alien encounters – Fiction	Pulp science fiction
Arthur Cheney Train and Robert Williams Wood	The Moon Maker	EN	1958	Science fiction	Novel – limited run published by Dawn Press
Mary T. Swickard	Apples in Appealing Ways	EN	1951	Cooking (Apples)	US Department of Agriculture leaflet 312

Catherine T. Byrce et a	Learning to Spell: A Manual for Teachers Using the Aldine Speller	EN	1921	Spellers – Textbooks	HathiTrust
Clair Price	The Rebirth of Turkey	EN	1923	Turkey – Politics and government	Internet Archive
Frances Trego Montgomery	Billy Whiskers at Home	EN	1924	Goats – Juvenile fiction	Internet Archive/ American Libraries

that volunteers can work with the original copies, such as a 1478 edition of Jean d'Arras's *Mélusine*. There are also clear patterns around historic race relations, which can be attributed to the renewed interested in the Black Lives Matter movement in 2020 after Derek Chauvin murdered George Floyd. Unfortunately, while this reveals a growing diversity in representation and content acquisition within PG's community, the list remains largely monolingual highlighting gaps in this coverage.

Regardless of the immediate future of Project Gutenberg, Hart's legacy will continue to be shaped by the mythology he developed over the course of the 1990s. Externally, PG represented an ideal digitisation imaginary while internally it showed the development of a community. The Frequently Asked Questions (FAQ) documents on the Project Gutenberg Literary Archive Foundation website are detailed, demonstrating the development of a consensus around core issues.[196] While in its early years, the Project may have claimed unique territory for digitising material that might not be available anywhere else, with the arrival of the Kindle, Google Books, the Internet Archive, HaithiTrust, and numerous other mass digitisation initiatives, PG would need to find a niche that distinguished itself from other platforms. This transformation was made possible by shifting focus from the volume of texts available – the Project would struggle to work at the same scale as others – but instead build an ecosystem for collaboration and interoperability. While this approach still led to blind spots, such as the gaps in coverage around gender and race, it transformed Project Gutenberg into sustainable infrastructure within the digitisation and digital humanities community that has continued to grow beyond Hart. As platforms and Web 2.0 hype enters its third decade, the resilience of collective-driven work such as PG offers a useful alternative.

---

[196] 'Gutenberg:Volunteers' FAQ'; 'Gutenberg:Copyright FAQ'.

Cast of Characters

Tim Berners-Lee	The inventor of the World Wide Web
Judy Boss	Professor of Native American Literature at Omaha University. Prolific early digitiser and proofreader for Project Gutenberg.
Lou Burnard	Co-founder of the Oxford Text Archive and prominent advocate for the Text Encoding Initiative.
Charles Frank	Founder of Distributed Proofreaders, a companion site to Project Gutenberg that speeds up the correction process.
Johannes Gutenberg	The inventor of the printing press within the European context
Hymen Hart	Michael Hart's father. A Professor of Shakespeare and World War II Cryptographer.
Michael Hart	Founder of Project Gutenberg.
Mary Brandt Jensen	Director of the University of San Diego Law Library and Project Gutenberg's Copyright Analyst.
Greg Newby	Professor at University of Illinois and long-time friend of Michael Hart. Founder of the Project Gutenberg Literary Archive Foundation.

Timeline

Bibliography

Abbate, Janet. *Inventing the Internet*. Cambridge: MIT Press, 2000.

Addams, Jane. *20 Years at Hull House [Project Gutenberg Book 1325]*. Edited by Project Gutenberg, 1998. https://gutenberg.org/files/1325/1325.txt.

Alighieri, Dante. *Divina Commedia Di Dante [Project Gutenberg Text 1000]*. Edited by Project Gutenberg, 1997. https://gutenberg.org/files/1000/old/1000.txt.

Ames, Morgan G. *The Charisma Machine: The Life, Death, and Legacy of One Laptop One Child*. Cambridge: MIT Press, 2019.

Arnold, Bruce. *The Scandal of Ulysses: The Life and Afterlife of a Twentieth Century Masterpiece*. 2nd ed. Dublin: The Liffey Press, 2004.

Arras, Jehan d'. *Mélusine [Project Gutenberg Book 65457]*. Edited by Distributed Proofreaders Team, 2021. www.gutenberg.org/files/65457/65457-h/65457-h.htm.

Barrie, James M. *Peter Pan [for US Only]** [Project Gutenberg Book 16]*. Edited by Project Gutenberg, 1991. https://gutenberg.org/files/16/old/peter16.txt.

Bean, Richard. 'The Use of Project Gutenberg and Hexagram Statistics to Help Solve Famous Unsolved Ciphers'. *Proceedings of the 3rd International Conference on Historical Cryptology HistoCrypt 2020* 171, no. 5 (19 May 2020): 31–5.

Berners-Lee, Tim. *Weaving the Web: The Past, Present and Future of the World Wide Web and Its Inventor*. London: Orion, 1999.

Bhushan, Abhay K. 'RFC 114: A File Transfer Perotocol'. IETF, 16 April 1971. https://tools.ietf.org/html/rfc114.

Bitzer, Donald L., Elisabeth R. Lyman, and John A. Easley Jr. 'The Uses of Plato: A Computer-Controlled Teaching System'. Washington, DC:

Clearinghouse for Federal Scientific and Technical Information, October 1965.

Bode, Katherine. 'The Equivalence of "Close" and "Distant" Reading; or, toward a New Object for Data-Rich Literary History'. *Modern Language Quarterly* 78, no. 1 (2017): 77–106.

Bourne, Charles P., and Trudi Bellardo Hahn. *A History of Online Information Services, 1963–1976*. Cambridge: MIT Press, 2003.

Brügger, Niels. 'Digital Humanities in the 21st Century: Digital Material as a Driving Force'. *Digital Humanities Quarterly* 10, no. 2 (2016). www .digitalhumanities.org/dhq/vol/10/3/000256/000256.html.

'Web Historiography and Internet Studies: Challenges and Perspectives'. *New Media & Society* 15, no. 5 (2013): 752–64.

Carlson, Gary. 'Literary Works in Machine-Readable Form'. *Computers and the Humanities* 1, no. 3 (1967): 75–102.

Carroll, Lewis. 'Alice's Adventures in Wonderland'. Project Gutenberg, 1994. www.gutenberg.org/files/11/old/alice30.txt.

Alice's Adventures in Wonderland [Project Gutenberg Book 11], 1994. www .gutenberg.org/files/11/old/.

Cassidy, Patrick J. 'MICRA Home Page'. MICRA, 17 May 2001. http:// web.archive.org/web/20010517213250/http://micra.com/.

Cisler, Steve. Letter to Kathy Askew. 'New Order [Project Gutenberg]', 19 November 1990. Series 4 Box 6 Folder 21. Apple Computer Inc Records 1977–1997 Corporate Library Misc Files.

Clerke, Agnes M. *Familiar Studies in Homer [Project Gutenberg Book 65000]*. Edited by Project Gutenberg, 2021. www.gutenberg.org/ebooks/ 65000.

Conan Doyle, Arthur. *Beyond the City [Project Gutenberg Book 356]*. Edited by Project Gutenberg, 1995. https://gutenberg.org/files/356/old/bcity10 .txt.

Cornell Chronicle. 'Joyce as Hypertext: The Digital Age Followed in His "Wake"', 22 June 2005. https://news.cornell.edu/stories/2005/06/joyce-hypertext-digital-age-followed-his-wake.

Creative Commons. 'About CC Licenses'. https://creativecommons.org/about/cclicenses/.

Csaky, Richard, and Gabor Recski. 'The Gutenberg Dialogue Dataset'. *ArXiv:2004.12752 [Cs]*, 22 January 2021. http://arxiv.org/abs/2004.12752.

Dame-Griff, Avery. 'Herding the "Performing Elephants": Using Computational Methods to Study Usenet'. *Internet Histories* 3, no. 3–4 (2019): 223–44.

'Directory of Scholars Active'. *Computers and the Humanities* 13, no. 4 (1979): 341–73.

Distributed Proofreaders. www.pgdp.net/c/.

Douglass, Frederick. 'Collected Articles of Frederick Douglass [Project Gutenberg Book 99]'. Project Gutenberg, 1994. https://gutenberg.org/ebooks/99.

DP Walkthrough – Introduction. www.pgdp.net/d/walkthrough/en/.

Driscoll, Kevin. *The Modem World: A Prehistory of Social Media*. New Haven: Yale University Press, 2022.

Eichmann-Kalwara, Nickoal, Scott B. Weingart, Matthew Lincoln, Camille Chidsey, and Heidi Wiren Bartlett. 'Association for Computers and the Humanities / International Conference on Computers and the Humanities'. Index of DH Conferences, 2021. https://dh-abstracts.library.cmu.edu/conference_series/2.

Eliot, George. *Middlemarch [Project Gutenberg Book 145]*, 1994. https://gutenberg.org/files/145/old/mdmar10.txt.

Epstein, Ralph. 'Industrial Invention: Heroic, or Systematic?' *The Quarterly Journal of Economics* 40, no. 2 (1926): 232–272

Founding Fathers. 'The Project Gutenberg Ebook of The United States' Constitution'. Project Gutenberg, 1975. http://gutenberg.org/files/5/old/constl1.txt.

Free Ebook Foundation Promotes Access and Preservation of Knowledge, Literature, and Culture. https://ebookfoundation.org/.

Fuller, Mark. Letter to Michael S. Hart. '1884–1890 Darby Bible (on Your Server Now)', 21 August 1992.

GameBoy Books to Go, 6 June 2004. http://web.archive.org/web/20040606220309/http://uk.geocities.com/ebooks2go/.

Genette, Gérard. *Palimpsests: Literature in the Second Degree.* Translated by Channa Newman and Claude Doubinsky. Lincoln: University of Nebraska Press, 1982.

Gerlach, Martin, and Francesc Font-Clos. 'A Standardized Project Gutenberg Corpus for Statistical Analysis of Natural Language and Quantitative Linguistics'. *Entropy* 22, no. 1 (2020): 126. https://doi.org/10.3390/e22010126.

Gillespie, Tarleton. 'The Politics of "Platforms"'. *New Media & Society* 12, no. 3 (2010): 347–64.

Goldstein, Gordon D. 'Plato II-University of Illinois, Urbana, Ill'. *Digital Computer Newsletter* 13, no. 4 (1961): 18–24.

Gorwa, Robert. 'What Is Platform Governance?' *Information, Communication & Society* 22, no. 6 (2019): 854–71.

Gregg, Stephen H. *Old Books and Digital Publishing: Eighteenth-Century Collections Online.* Cambridge: Cambridge University Press, 2020.

Grier, David A., and Mary Campbell. 'A Social History of Bitnet and Listserv, 1985–1991'. *IEEE Annals of the History of Computing* 22, no. 2 (April 2000): 32–41.

Grimes, William. 'Michael Hart, a Pioneer of E-Books, Dies at 64'. New York Times, 8 September 2011. http://web.archive.org/web/

20220318094827/https://www.nytimes.com/2011/09/09/business/michael-hart-a-pioneer-of-e-books-dies-at-64.html.

Hamilton, Denise. 'Hart of the Gutenberg Galaxy'. *WIRED*, February 1997. www.wired.com/1997/02/esgutenberg/.

Hart, Hymen Harold. 'Edward Capell: The First Modern Editor of Shakespeare'. Ph.D, University of Illinois, 1967.

Hart, Michael. 'More Shakespeare and Other Machine-Readable Texts Available'. *Off-Line* 17, no. 4 (October 1989): 6–7.

    Letter to Monica Ertel 'Request for Mac and Scanner [Bitmail]', 22 October 1990. Series 4 Box 6 Folder 21. Apple Computer Inc Records 1977–1997 Corporate Library Misc Files.

Hart, Michael, and Greg Newby. 'Project Gutenberg Principle of Minimal Regulation/ Administration'. Project Gutenberg, 2004. https://gutenberg.org/about/background/minimal_regulation.html.

Hart, Michael S. 'First.Million.Ebooks.Txt'. Michael S. Hart Archives (Born Digital), 10 October 2006. https://archives.library.illinois.edu/e-records/index.php?dir=University%20Archives/2620191/political_creative_writings/Accession2/ARTICLES/SAVING%20THE%20WORLD/.

    'Mt.Specifics.Txt'. Michael S. Hart Archives (Born Digital), 29 April 2007. https://archives.library.illinois.edu/e-records/index.php?dir=University%20Archives/2620191/political_creative_writings/Accession2/ARTICLES/SAVING%20THE%20WORLD/.

    'Prizes.Txt'. Michael S. Hart Archives (Born Digital), 8 April 2008. https://archives.library.illinois.edu/erec/University%20Archives/2620191/project_gutenberg/Accession2/PROJECTS/prizes.txt.

    'Service Mark Principal Register: Project Gutenberg'. USPTO TSDR Case Viewer, 2000. https://tsdr.uspto.gov/documentviewer?caseId=sn76155278&docId=SPE20001026000000#docIndex=9&page=1.

'The History and Philosophy of Project Gutenberg', Project Gutenberg, 1992. www.gutenberg.org/about/background/history_and_philosophy .html.

'Who.Invented.Ebooks.Txt'. Michael S. Hart Archives (Born Digital), 3 October 2006. https://archives.library.illinois.edu/e-records/ index.php?dir=University%20Archives/2620191/political_creative_ writings/Accession2/ARTICLES/SAVING%20THE%20 WORLD/.

Heart, Frank, Alexander McKenzie, John McQuillan, and David Walden. 'A History of the ARPANET: The First Decade'. Arlington: Defense Advanced Research Projects Agency, 1 April 1981. https://apps.dtic .mil/dtic/tr/fulltext/u2/a115440.pdf.

Hockey, Susan. 'The History of Humanities Computing'. In *A Companion to Digital Humanities*, edited by Susan Schreibman, Ray Siemens, and John Unsworth, 3–19. Oxford: Blackwell, 2004. www.digitalhuma nities.org/companion/.

Hodgson Burnett, Frances. *The Secret Garden [Project Gutenberg Book 113]*. Edited by Project Gutenberg, 1994. https://gutenberg.org/files/ 113/old/gardn10.txt.

Irving, Washington. *The Legend of Sleepy Hollow [Project Gutenberg Book 41]*, 1992. https://gutenberg.org/files/41/old/sleep10.txt.

Jiang, Ming, Yuerong Hu, Glen Worthey et al. 'The Gutenberg-HathiTrust Parallel Corpus: A Real-World Dataset for Noise Investigation in Uncorrected OCR Texts', 17 March 2021. www.ideals.illinois.edu/ handle/2142/109695.

Johns, Adrian. *The Nature of the Book: Print and Knowledge in the Making*. Chicago: The University of Chicago Press, 1998.

Joyce, James. *Ulysses [Project Gutenberg Book 4300]*. Edited by Project Gutenberg, 2003. https://gutenberg.org/ebooks/4300.

Kennedy, Thomas Gordon. 'GATT-out of the Public Domain: Constitutional Dimensions of Foreign Copyright Restoration Note'. *St. John's Journal of Legal Commentary* 11, no. 2 (1995–1996): 545–80.

Kilgour, Frederick. *The Evolution of the Book*. New York: Oxford University Press, 1998.

Kirschenbaum, Matthew G. 'The Txtual Condition: Digital Humanities, Born-Digital Archives, and the Future Literary'. *Digital Humanities Quarterly* 7, no. 1 (2013). www.digitalhumanities.org/dhq/vol/7/1/ 000151/000151.html.

Langdon, John. 'Describing the Digital: The Archival Cataloguing of Born-Digital Personal Papers'. *Archives and Records* 37, no. 1 (2016): 37–52.

Lisi Rankin, Joy. *A People's History of Computing in the United States*. Cambridge: Harvard University Press, 2018.

LOCKSS. www.lockss.org/.

Mak, Bonnie. 'Archaeology of a Digitization'. *Journal of the Association for Information Science and Technology* 65, no. 8 (2014): 1515–26.

Maxwell, John. 'Coach House Press in the "Early Digital" Period: A Celebration'. *Devil's Artisan: A Journal of the Printing Arts* 77 (2015): 9–20.

McCahill, Mark, Paul Lindner, Daniel Torrey et al. 'RFC 1436: The Internet Gopher Protocol (a Distributed Document Search and Retrieval Protocol)', March 1993. https://tools.ietf.org/html/ rfc1436.

Melanchthon, Philipp. *Die Augsburger Confession [Project Gutenberg Book 607]*. Edited by Project Gutenberg, 1996. www.gutenberg.org/ ebooks/607.

Merton, Robert. 'Singletons and Multiples in Scientific Discovery: A Chapter in the Sociology of Science'. *Proceedings of the American Philosophical Society* 105, no. 5 (1961): 470–86.

Montfort, Nick, Patsy Baudoin, John Bell et al. *10 PRINT CHR$(205.5+ RND(1));: GOTO 10*. Cambridge: MIT Press, 2012.

Montfort, Nick, and Ian Bogost. *Racing the Beam: The Atari Video Computer System*. Cambridge: MIT Press, 2009.

Morrison, Alan. 'Delivering Electronic Texts over the Web: The Current and Planned Practices of the Oxford Text Archive'. *Computers and the Humanities* 33 (1999): 193–8.

Mullaney, Thomas S. *The Chinese Typewriter*. Cambridge: MIT Press, 2017.

Murphy, Andrew. *Shakespeare in Print: A History and Chronology of Shakespeare Publishing*. Cambridge: Cambridge University Press, 2021.

Neuman, Michael. 'The Very Pulse of the Machine: Three Trends toward Improvement in Electronic Versions of Humanities Texts'. *Computers and the Humanities* 25 (1991): 363–75.The New York Public Library. 'Generative EBook Covers'. www.nypl.org/blog/2014/09/03/gen erative-ebook-covers.

Northeastern University Women Writers Project. 'WWP History'. Women Writers Project, 2021. www.wwp.northeastern.edu/about/ history/.

Ockerbloom, Mary Mark. 'A Celebration of Women Writers'. A Celebration of Women Writers, 2020. http://digital.library.upenn.edu/women/.

Office of University Relations. 'Memorial Service to Honor Hymen Hart'. *MU NewsLetter* 109 (8 February 1990): 2.

'Promotion and Tenure'. *Marshall University News Letter* 492 (20 April 1981): 1.

Olson, Mark. 'Webster Search Form'. ARTFL Project, 4 December 1996. http://web.archive.org/web/19961204135512/ http://humanities .uchicago.edu/forms_unrest/webster.form.html.

Oomen, Johan, and Lora Aroyo. 'Crowdsourcing in the Cultural Heritage Domain: Opportunities and Challenges'. In *Proceedings of the 5th*

International Conference on Communities and Technologies, 138–49. New York: Association for Computing Machinery, 2011.

Özdemir, Lale. 'The Inevitability of Digital Transfer: How Prepared are UK Public Bodies for the Transfer of Born-Digital Records to the Archives?' *Records Management Journal* 29, no. 1/2 (1 January 2019): 224–39.

Pargman, Daniel, and Jacob Palme. 'ASCII Imperialism'. In *Standards and Their Stories: How Quantifying, Classifying and Formalizing Practices Shape Everyday Life*, edited by Martha Lampland and Susan Leigh Star, 177–99. Ithaca: Cornell University Press, 2009.

Parnell, Claire. 'Mapping the Entertainment Ecosystem of Wattpad: Platforms, Publishing and Adaptation'. *Convergence* 27, no. 2 (2021): 524–38.

Pechenick, Eitan Adam, Christopher M. Danforth, and Peter Sheridan Dodds. 'Characterizing the Google Books Corpus: Strong Limits to Inferences of Socio-Cultural and Linguistic Evolution'. *PLOS ONE* 10, no. 10 (2015): 1–24. https://doi.org/10.1371/journal.pone.0137041.

Peters, Benjamin. 'A Network Is Not a Network'. In *Your Computer Is on Fire*, edited by Thomas S. Mullaney, Benjamin Peters, Mar Hicks, and Kavita Philip, 71–90. Cambridge: MIT Press, 2021.

Peters, Justin. *The Idealist: Aaron Swartz and the Rise of Free Culture on the Internet*. London: Duckworth Overlook, 2017.

Pettitt, Tom. 'Before the Gutenberg Parenthesis: Elizabethan-American Compatibilities'. In *Media in Transition 5: Creativity, Ownership and Collaboration in the Digital Age*, n.d. http://web.mit.edu/comm-forum/mit5/papers/pettitt_plenary_gutenberg.pdf.

PGLAF. 'Cease and Desist Responses' *Project Gutenberg Literary Archive Foundation*. https://cand.pglaf.org/

Poynder, Richard, and Michael Hart. 'Preserving the Public Domain'. The Basement Interviews, 2006. https://ia803403.us.archive.org/28/items/The_Basement_Interviews/Michael_Hart_Interview.pdf.

Project Gutenberg, ed. *Bibeln, Gamla Och Nya Testamentet [Project Gutenberg Book 2100]*, 2000. www.gutenberg.org/ebooks/2100.

King James Bible [Project Gutenberg Text 10], 1989. https://gutenberg.org/files/10/old/.

Project Gutenberg. 'Gutenberg: Copyright FAQ', 30 August 2006. http://web.archive.org/web/20060830202603/, www.gutenberg.org/wiki/Gutenberg:Copyright_FAQ.

Project Gutenberg. 'Gutenberg: Volunteers' FAQ', 30 August 2006. http://web.archive.org/web/20060830202538/, www.gutenberg.org/wiki/Gutenberg:Volunteers%27_FAQ.

Project Gutenberg. 'The Declaration of Independence of the United States of America by Thomas Jefferson', 3 January 2018. http://webarchive.loc.gov/all/20180103200450/, www.gutenberg.org/ebooks/1.

Project Runeberg. http://runeberg.org/.

Ramdarshan Bold, Melanie. 'The Return of the Social Author: Negotiating Authority and Influence on Wattpad'. *Convergence* 24, no. 2 (2018): 117–36.

Randell, Brian 'The Origins of Computer Programming'. *IEEE Annals of the History of Computing* 16, no. 4 (Winter 1994): 6–14.

Rice Burroughs, Edgar. *Tarzan and the Jewel of Opar [Project Gutenberg Book 92]*. Edited by Project Gutenberg, 1993. https://gutenberg.org/files/92/old/tarz510.txt.

Richardson, Leonard. 'Project Gutenberg Books are Real'. *Journal of Electronic Publishing* 18, no. 1 (2015). https://doi.org/10.3998/3336451.0018.126.

Ridge, Mia. *Crowdsourcing Our Cultural Heritage*. Farnham: Ashgate, 2014.

Roberts, Sarah T. *Beyond the Screen: Content Moderation in the Shadows of Social Media*. New Haven: Yale University Press, 2019.

Rowberry, Simon Peter. *Four Shades of Gray: The Amazon Kindle Platform*. Cambridge: MIT Press, 2022.

Shloss, Carol Loeb. 'Joyce's Will'. *NOVEL: A Forum on Fiction* 29, no. 1 (1995): 114–27.

Silberman, Steve. 'A Thousand Classics for the ASCIIng'. WIRED, 11 June 1997. www.wired.com/1997/06/a-thousand-classics-for-the-asciing/.

Simonton, Dean Keith. 'Multiple Discovery and Invention: Zeitgeist, Genius, or Chance?' *Journal of Personality and Social Psychology* 37, no. 9 (1979): 1603–1616.

Smith, Robert E. 'What Is Project Wittenberg?' Project Wittenberg, 1996. www.projectwittenberg.org/pub/resources/text/wittenberg/about-wittenberg.txt.

Spoo, Robert. *Without Copyrights: Piracy, Publishing, and the Public Domain*. Oxford: Oxford University Press, 2013.

Stanford Literary Lab. https://litlab.stanford.edu/.

Streeter, Tom. *The Net Effect: Romanticism, Capitalism, and the Internet*. Cambridge: MIT Press, 2010.

Summerhayes, Martha. *Vanished Arizona [Project Gutenberg Book 1049]*. Edited by Project Gutenberg, 1997. https://gutenberg.org/files/1049/old/variz10.txt.

W3C. 'Tags Used in HTML', 1992. www.w3.org/History/19921103-hypertext/hypertext/WWW/MarkUp/Tags.html.

Tenneshaw, S. M. 'Kill Me If You Can! [Project Gutenberg Book 65451]'. Edited by Distributed Proofreaders team. *Imagination Stories of Science and Fantasy*, June 1957. www.gutenberg.org/files/65451/65451-h/65451-h.htm.

Terras, Melissa. 'Digital Curiosities: Resource Creation via Amateur Digitization'. *Literary and Linguistic Computing* 25, no. 4 (2010): 425–38.

Terras, Melissa, and Julianne Nyhan. 'Father Busa's Female Punch Card Operatives'. In *Debates in the Digital Humanities 2016*, edited by

Matthew K. Gold and Lauren F. Klein, 60–65. Minneapolis: University of Minnesota Press, 2016.

Thylstrup, Nanna Bonde. *The Politics of Mass Digitization*. Cambridge: MIT Press, 2019.

Trettien, Whitney Anne. 'A Deep History of Electronic Textuality: The Case of English Reprints John Milton *Areopagitica*'. *Digital Humanities Quarterly* 7, no. 1 (2013). www.digitalhumanities.org/dhq/vol/7/1/000150/000150.html.

Turner, Fred. *From Counterculture to Cyberculture: Stewart Brand, the Whole Earth Network, and the Rise of Digital Utopianism*. Chicago: The University of Chicago Press, 2006.

U.S. Copyright Office. 'Notices of Restored Copyrights', 2019. www.copyright.gov/gatt.html.

USPTO. '2141 Examination Guidelines for Determining Obviousness under 35 U.S.C. 103 [R-10.2019]', 2019. www.uspto.gov/web/offices/pac/mpep/s2141.html.

Vaknin, Sam. 'The Ubiquitous Project Gutenberg: Interview with Michael Hart, Its Founder'. Sam Vak, 15 November 2005. http://samvak.tripod.com/busiweb46.html.

Wattpad. 'Gutenberg', 2007. www.wattpad.com/user/gutenberg.

Weber, Millicent. '"Reading" the Public Domain: Narrating and Listening to Librivox Audiobooks'. *Book History* 24, no. 1 (2021): 209–43.

Webster, Noah. *The Gutenberg Webster's Unabridged Dictionary: Section A and B*, 1996. http://gutenberg.org/files/660/old/pgwab04.txt.

Woodworth, Seth. 'GITenberg'. GitHub, 2014. https://github.com/GITenberg.

Acknowledgements

This research was made possible by the generous funding of the Bibliographical Society of America's McCorison Fellowship for the History and Bibliography of Printing in Canada and the United States award and a Carnegie Trust Research Initiative Grant to visit relevant archives.

Cambridge Elements ≡

Publishing and Book Culture

SERIES EDITOR
Samantha Rayner
University College London

Samantha Rayner is Professor of Publishing and Book Cultures at UCL. She is also Director of UCL's Centre for Publishing, co-Director of the Bloomsbury CHAPTER (Communication History, Authorship, Publishing, Textual Editing and Reading) and co-Chair of the Bookselling Research Network.

ASSOCIATE EDITOR
Leah Tether
University of Bristol

Leah Tether is Professor of Medieval Literature and Publishing at the University of Bristol. With an academic background in medieval French and English literature and a professional background in trade publishing, Leah has combined her expertise and developed an international research profile in book and publishing history from manuscript to digital.

About the Series

This series aims to fill the demand for easily accessible, quality texts available for teaching and research in the diverse and dynamic fields of Publishing and Book Culture. Rigorously researched and peer-reviewed Elements will be published under themes, or 'Gatherings'. These Elements should be the first check point for researchers or students working on that area of publishing and book trade history and practice: we hope that, situated so logically at Cambridge University Press, where academic publishing in the UK began, it will develop to create an unrivalled space where these histories and practices can be investigated and preserved.

Cambridge Elements ≡

Publishing and Book Culture
Digital Literary Culture

Gathering Editor: Laura Dietz

Laura Dietz is a Senior Lecturer in Writing and Publishing in
the Cambridge School of Creative Industries at Anglia Ruskin
University. She writes novels and studies novels, publishing
fiction alongside research on topics such as e-novel readership,
the digital short story, online literary magazines, and the
changing definition of authorship in the digital era.

ELEMENTS IN THE GATHERING

A full series listing is available at: www.cambridge.org/EPBC

Printed in the United States
by Baker & Taylor Publisher Services